Dear Reader:

P9-DDN-895

The book you are about to read is the latest bestseller from the St. Martin's True Crime Library, the imprint *The New York Times* calls "the leader in true crime!" Each month, we offer you a fascinating account of the latest, most sensational crime that has captured the national attention. St. Martin's is the publisher of bestselling true crime author and crime journalist Kieran Crowley, who explores the dark, deadly links between a prominent Manhattan surgeon and the disappearance of his wife fifteen years earlier in THE SURGEON'S WIFE. Suzy Spencer's BREAKING POINT guides readers through the tortuous twists and turns in the case of Andrea Yates, the Houston mother who drowned her five young children in the family's bathtub. In Edgar Award-nominated DARK DREAMS, legendary FBI profiler Roy Hazelwood and bestselling crime author Stephen G. Michaud shine light on the inner workings of America's most violent and depraved murderers. In the book you now hold, BONES IN THE DESERT, acclaimed author Jana Bommersbach explores a daughter's search for her missing mother.

St. Martin's True Crime Library gives you the stories behind the headlines. Our authors take you right to the scene of the crime and into the minds of the most notorious murderers to show you what really makes them tick. St. Martin's True Crime Library paperbacks are better than the most terrifying thriller, because it's all true! The next time you want a crackling good read, make sure it's got the St. Martin's True Crime Library logo on the spine—you'll be up all night!

Charles E. Spicer, Jr.
Executive Editor, St. Martin's True Crime Library

BONES
IN THE DESERT

The True Story of a Mother's Murder and a Daughter's Search

JANA BOMMERSBACH

St. Martin's Paperbacks

BONES IN THE DESERT

Copyright © 2008 by Jana Bommersbach.

Cover photo of Loretta Bowersock courtesy of Terri Bowersock. Cover photo of background image © Getty Images.

For information address St. Martin's Press, 175 Fifth Avenue, New York, NY 10010.

ISBN: 0-312-94741-0
EAN: 978-0-312-94741-5

Printed in the United States of America

St. Martin's Paperbacks edition / October 2008

St. Martin's Paperbacks are published by St. Martin's Press, 175 Fifth Avenue, New York, NY 10010.

10 9 8 7 6 5 4 3

This book is dedicated to my family, who taught me what family love is all about and have never wavered in their faith and love: Rudy, Willie, Judy, Gary and Susan, Duane and Jeanette, Keith and Craig.

TABLE OF CONTENTS

ix   Acknowledgments

1   Prologue

7   Chapter One: *The Last Week*

39   Chapter Two: *Getting Rid of Loretta*

59   Chapter Three: *The Early Years*

80   Chapter Four: *Your Mother's Missing*

98   Chapter Five: *Secrets at Home*

105   Chapter Six: *Burying Loretta*

110   Chapter Seven: *Splitting Mother and Daughter*

121   Chapter Eight: *A Motive for Murder*

133   Chapter Nine: *The End of Taw*

160   Chapter Ten: *Horrible Discoveries*

181   Chapter Eleven: *The Media*

201   Chapter Twelve: *The Psychics*

215   Chapter Thirteen: *Searching the Desert*

227   Chapter Fourteen: *Finding the Body*

241   Chapter Fifteen: *We Have Found Your Mother*

252   Chapter Sixteen: *A New Start*

270   Epilogue

ACKNOWLEDGMENTS

THANKS: There are so many people who helped make this book possible.

First is Robert Stieve, my former editor at *Phoenix* magazine, who supported the telling of this story from the start, as well as Bill Phalen, chairman of the board of the magazine. My agent, Nat Sobel, saw the importance of this story for a book, and my wonderful editor at St. Martin's Press, Michael Homler, helped make it a reality. I'll always be grateful for the help from Sergeant Dan Masters of the Tempe Police Department, along with all the other officers who so generously gave me their time, files and memories of this case.

My dear friends, Marge Injasoulian and Barb Hanson were there every step of the way, with their insights and wisdom, and Marge Rice provided invaluable editing and encouragement. Thanks also to Gail Adams, Jay Goodfarb, Jim and Linda Ballenger, Robert Ehmann, Dr. Rob Jones, Athia Hardt, Cathy Eden, Nan and Dave Robb, Tommy Martinez, Ken Smith, Mary Margaret and John Sather, Francesca Bianco,

Maxine Beckstrom, Terry and Julie Lehnis and the late Shirlee Lehnis.

Warm thanks to my new Brainerd friends, including Nancy Neptune, who made so many wonderful things happen; the Lindroth family, Art, JoAnn, Diane and Gary; fellow writer Wendy Rosnau; summer neighbor Shirley Andreason; my YMCA buddies, Mary Sieling, Karen Johnson and Chris Larson; Johnny at Elite Nails, and Lisa at A Cut Above.

But most of all I have to thank Terri Bowersock for opening up her heart, her memories and her mother's papers so this story could be told. Reliving it all over again had to be painful, but she never failed to face the challenge. She is a devoted daughter and because of her, her mother's memory will live forever.

PROLOGUE

It's one of those cute pictures you blow up and frame because it's not only flattering, but shows such a happy couple at such a happy moment.

The picture was taken on an Alaskan cruise, just before another scrumptious feast, in November of 2004.

Loretta Bowersock's beautiful smile fills her pretty face as she snuggles next to her handsome man—she calls him her husband, but she and Taw Benderly have never legally tied the knot in all the eighteen years they've been together.

You'd never know that from this picture, snapped by Loretta's daughter, Terri, who treated them to this amazing cruise.

Their body language is so intimate, you can imagine they shared a kiss after the camera finished. And you just know they're going to show off this snapshot to everyone who visits their happy home.

Who could possibly believe that within a month of this picture, that man would kill that woman?

This is not a typical murder story. Not from where it happened, to how it happened, to why it happened to someone you'd never dream it could happen to. And certainly there isn't usually the grisly aftermath of a murder without a body—a body thought stashed somewhere in the vast Sonoran Desert around Phoenix; a body with no proper resting place where loved ones could come to grieve; a missing body that prompted a thirteen-month search and fears that beautiful 69-year-old Loretta Bowersock had ended up a coyote's evening meal.

Murder doesn't get more personal than this one, which shocked the 48th State just before Christmas in 2004—losing a beautiful, successful businesswoman and mother of the state's "Domestic Diva." Over the last quarter century, the mother-daughter team of Loretta and Terri Bowersock had gone from rags to riches in front of everyone's eyes, and become one of Arizona's favorite triumphs. They were television commercial stars—ads they wrote and acted in themselves—touting the "gently used" furniture of a new type of consignment business that made them rich. And their background story was so compelling: Terri became a nationally celebrated darling, winning coveted business awards and featured on *Oprah*. Dyslexia hadn't stopped Terri from becoming a millionaire, Oprah gushed, even though "she couldn't even fill out a job application." Terri only made it with the help of her mom and a loan from her grandma. It was a true American success story.

Now here was such an ugly chapter. Most people never know a murder victim, but this time, almost everyone in Arizona did. For many, this felt like a murder in the family. The state's media covered the story as though Terri were their mourning sister—hanging with her long after police stopped searching.

Her other lifeline was a herd of psychics, who

flocked to this case almost instantly. They came in person, over the phone, by letters, by emails. They came with their "visions" of the murder and "maps" of the burial site. They came recounting "conversations" they'd had with Loretta. And they eventually came with anguished utterances from Taw before he "crossed over." Terri clung to their every word, keeping the faith that they really could see something; that they really were hearing Loretta give them clues on where to find her. Some thought Terri was nuts to be so taken in, but two police officers would later admit that at least one psychic had indeed helped the case, and the national TV show, *Psychic Detectives*, would crow about it.

In the meantime, hundreds of condolence cards, letters and emails came into Terri's home and office, as the nation reached out to comfort her.

"I just wanted you to know many, many people are thinking about you and praying for you," Rosie wrote. Craig Stull called to say he owned a helicopter and would help search the desert. "I can't stop crying, it is sooo sad what happened to your mom," wrote Tanya. Janet and Paul said they were in town on vacation, but wanted to help search. Customers stopped in the four consignment stores to tell the clerks how devastated they were. Church people put Loretta on their prayer lists. One little boy wrote saying he couldn't imagine how much pain she must be in, losing a mom and not knowing where she was.

None of them had any idea of the depth of Terri's anguish. Because there was so much more than appeared on the surface.

This isn't just the tragic story of a daughter losing

her mother in the worst possible way. This is the heartbreaking story of a grown child searching in death for a mother she'd already lost in life—a daughter who had seen her mother's betrayal and felt the sting of rejection, all for the man who moved into her mother's home and heart, and pushed aside everyone else. The rip in their relationship had been so painful and ugly, Terri felt as though Loretta had "died" long before the murder. The two had spent years trying to mend their lives, and just now, just in the last few months, things had gotten so much better. They'd had such fun on the Alaskan cruise. And then, unbelievably, it was all over.

Still, it's impossible to stand in front of Loretta's one-story brick house in Tempe, with its pillars, double garage and red front door, and imagine any of this happening. This is how most of Arizona lives, in nice neighborhoods with neat grass lawns and oleander bushes that bloom in winter. This is where sane people live, safe people have dinner, secure families make lives.

Loretta Bowersock had lived here almost thirty years, buying it for a song, and watching it skyrocket in value to a nice nest egg she could count on. She intended to spend her last days here.

The sad thing is, she did. But Loretta didn't leave her beautiful home from the red front door, which was already festooned with a Christmas wreath that December day in 2004.

She left wrapped in black landscaping tarp, ducttaped shut around her throat, her chest, her legs. But nobody would discover that for a very long time. Taw would insist that she'd just gone missing on a

Tucson shopping spree and he had no idea what happened to her.

This man, who thought he was the smartest guy on the planet and "could talk snow off a snowball," spent his last days bitterly complaining that police were after him, like he was some Scott Peterson killer or something, and how could they think that? He even shed tears. His death came at his own hand, and all the secrets he knew about Loretta went to hell with him.

But he wasn't done, even then, torturing everyone who'd ever loved Loretta—her daughter, her son in Hawaii, her three surviving sisters, the love of her life who'd slipped away, her many girlfriends.

As Terri emptied her mother's house, she discovered a shocking life she'd never guessed was lived here. The remnants Loretta and Taw left behind showed that the cute picture was a lie—this was not a happy home with a loving couple, but a house of despair and abuse, of anger and conflict, of cheating and stealing and forging and defrauding.

And what Terri read in her mother's private journals—page after page of Loretta's most intimate thoughts and fears—broke her heart.

Terri was about to learn her mother was a "classic case of elder abuse." Loretta fit the awful pattern to a *T*. Some had seen it coming, but either couldn't or wouldn't stop it. "We were raised to keep peace in the family at any cost," one sister would say. Loretta's price had been to stay out of her business. It's a far too familiar story to far too many American families.

Terri is now determined her mother won't end up just another statistic. She's created a new business to raise money to help other women escape from the clutches of elder abuse.

Terri wants women like her mother to know there's an alternative—women from the generation that can't stand to face their senior years alone; lonely women who believe they're better off with a bad man than no man at all.

By the time Loretta Bowersock realized how wrong that was, she'd run out of time to save herself.

This is the inside story.

CHAPTER 1

The Last Week

The last week of Loretta Bowersock's life started out joyously—a blessing to the middle of five daughters who was remembered at her mother's funeral as the "joyous" one.

On this Tuesday, December 7, 2004, Loretta was 69 years old, but still had the tennis-pro figure of her earlier years, carrying just 130 pounds on her 5-foot-6-inch frame. She still dressed like the "fashion queen" she'd been for decades, and showed so few signs of aging that nobody would have guessed she was about to enter her seventies.

If you wanted a fun person—someone with a constant smile on her face and a swing in her walk—then Loretta came immediately to mind. Her sisters would always remember her as "energetic and very generous," if not headstrong and determined to do things her own way. She entered the world on March 2, 1935, and was a particularly happy baby. And she carried that with her through the years. She showed a flair for dressing up and presenting all her good points to advantage early on, just as she danced about the best jitterbug anyone can remember from her days growing up in Kansas as Loretta Jean McJilton.

The girlfriends she met along the way—women

who would remain her friends for decades—always thought of her as "Miss Personality." She could talk with anyone about almost anything. She was interested in politics and current affairs, in sports and business, in bridge and gourmet cooking. She paid attention to the news going on in Tempe, the Arizona town she'd called home for decades, which sits next to Arizona's largest city and capital, Phoenix. She was always trying to improve herself and her mind, and if you suggested something new, girlfriends would recall, she'd be the first in line to learn. Her easy and attractive ways made her a magnet at the bars she and friends visited in their forties as they looked for, but never found, second husbands.

"A classy lady" always started a long list of accolades from her only daughter, although if you listened long enough, eventually Terri would get to her one complaint about her mom: "Her generation believes women should stand by their men and live in houses with white picket fences—she's afraid to be alone without a man."

She was an "outgoing woman who wouldn't take crap," her son, Scott, adds.

Loretta labeled herself an extrovert, but acknowledged that she was an old-fashioned woman. Her life had been a series of mixed signals. She fought for control over her teen years with her father—bullheadedly defying his rules. She would do things her way, she'd tell him, and the constant conflict in the household got pretty thick sometimes. Nor would she listen to her older sisters when they tried to give her advice. Like when they warned her that a handsome airman named Dave Bowersock was just too old for her. He should have been after one of her older sisters, but it was Loretta who caught his eye. Nobody in the family was very thrilled about it, except Loretta, who married him and went off to live around the country for the next nineteen years as a dutiful wife of an Air Force officer.

"She really relished that role," remembers Terri, who was in her mid-teens when her parents divorced. "You could just see her playing the role. At Christmas we had a full-blown tree and all the trimmings, and everything was always just perfect, and you could just hear her saying, 'This is what an officer's wife should be doing,' and she thought it was *Leave It to Beaver.*"

It seemed the perfect family: a handsome man in uniform, a beautiful woman in her lovely home, a son, a daughter—but it wouldn't be the first time a family kept up the appearances. Loretta doted on her son, Scott, who was the first born, while daughter Terri always felt second best. "My mother comes from a family of five sisters, so when my brother came along, she was in love—she had a boy! When I came along, it was just another girl, and I was a crying baby, so that didn't help."

"About everybody knew I was the favorite," Scott admits, "but I was the kid who wasn't any trouble. Terri was a needy, noisy kid. I'm more introverted. I'd come home after school and go to my room to listen to music. Terri would come home bouncing off the walls." To this day, he admits that "she's my sister and I love her, but I don't have anything in common with her."

Loretta hung on to the marriage until she couldn't

hang on any longer, and by then, she was living in Arizona. Now she had to take control of her own life, whether she wanted to or not. The failure of her marriage clearly shook her—"We watched her change," Terri remembers—and Loretta started serial dating, younger men, older men, all kinds of men. But none of them stuck. Most didn't meet her expectations; some didn't want such a needy woman.

Soon, Scott was off studying psychology and Terri was finishing her high school years and demanding independence; Loretta, for the first time, had time to focus on her own needs.

The great irony is that at this very moment, she proved that she was perfectly capable of taking care of herself. In fact, she began the most productive period of her life. At 37, she earned a college degree from Arizona State University. She started teaching dance, then tennis; she became a tennis pro; she opened two businesses, and each step along that route had meant bigger and better things. She had made enough money on her own—by her own wits, personality and skill—to fill her hands with jewels and buy a beautiful home.

But as well as she was faring on her own, Loretta still yearned for a man in her life. And one day, in response to an advertisement renting out her guest bedroom, one arrived like some modern Galahad, with a motorcycle for a steed.

Taw Benderly had been a knock-out—in today's parlance, a "hottie"—when he'd first arrived on her doorstep, and even at 66, he still cut a fine figure. He was tall and handsome, intelligent and well-spoken, a great cook and an expert in art glass. He had an MBA from the Wharton School of Business, just like his classmate Donald Trump, and was an inventor who knew just about anything about everything. He had a mesmerizing voice and spoke with such authority that few challenged him. You didn't spend ten minutes in his presence without knowing he thought he was smarter than anyone in the room, and that he had an unflagging confidence in himself and the inventions that would someday make him rich. He and Loretta made a very good-looking couple. From what everyone saw, they'd spend all their remaining years together.

To anyone looking in, Loretta was the kind of accomplished, secure woman who was living out her senior years in good health and good form, and had the kind of solid middle-class life anyone of that age would envy. She was bright and active, belonged to a bridge club, had a loving family, and friends she'd kept for decades. She had a daughter who was a local media star, called "the Domestic Diva," which gave Loretta a dose of celebrity, too. Her son and his wife lived in Hawaii, and all seemed fine there. She'd lost one sister to cancer, but was in close contact with the other three, and she loved writing long emails to her loving nieces and nephews.

So it would have seemed that a joyous week wasn't that unusual for a woman who had so much ⌐ live for. But that was just the public front of her
    In reality, most of that was a façade. No, the joy-
    start of her final week was so delightful because
    wasn't an emotion often found inside her ranch

house on Tempe's Manhattan Drive. This wasn't a
fine home with a happy couple and a busy social life.
This was a home where fear and anger were more
common, a home where the number one anxiety was
financial insecurity.

In every list Loretta ever made about her fears—
in her constant self-improvement quests, she visited
this question again and again—the top fear was always the same: She'd grown up with an oilman father who struck dirt most of the time, but was always
blustering about the big score just down the next
hole. "Someday, coming around the corner will be a
white Cadillac," Luther McJilton would say. Yes, her
father did eventually strike oil, but that was late in
the game, and Loretta remembered a childhood of financial disappointment. She also well knew it was
mother Gladys's real estate company that kept them
afloat, and she vowed as a girl that she wanted a solid
provider at her side, not some fly-by-night dreamer
with no respect for the value of a dollar.

So it astonished even her that she'd landed herself in the same situation as her childhood, with a
boyfriend who always dreamed his version of the
white Cadillac but never brought home the keys.

That's certainly not how she'd expected this story
to end when he'd roared up on a motorcycle eighteen
years ago. She'd had such high hopes when he answered an ad that Terri had encouraged her to run:
"Executive woman, big home, nice suite for ren
Loretta's house was perfectly suited for a renter, v
the master bedroom suite on one end and a guest
room and bath at the other. She'd had a couple ren
in the past and had not only liked the company, but th

extra money helped with the household expenses. Loretta clearly did not like living alone.

Taw arrived straddling a Harley, with no billfold, no suitcase and no money in his jeans. He said he'd just flown in from Saudi Arabia, where he'd worked for Bechtel. Everything had gone wrong: the company had lost his last paycheck, his wallet had been stolen at the airport and his luggage had gotten lost in transit. But he was an inventor with a big idea that was going to make him so much money someday, he'd never live long enough to spend it all. He couldn't pay any rent until that lost check turned up, but until then, he would help out—he was a gourmet cook and could fix almost anything. And if she'd trust him for the rent, he'd cut her in on his invention when it came through, and they'd both be rich.

As implausible as all that sounds, Loretta fell for it. To her, it was exciting and exotic and hypnotic. Anyone who's ever read a romance novel will see the familiar plot: big, handsome man comes to save you, but he needs rescuing, too, and you're just the woman to do it. Somebody needs to believe in him—to support him and stand by him. And the gamble you take will pay off in riches and love ever after, and all the lonely days will be over. It's a high-school view of life, but it's one that has made romance novels the biggest-selling book category in the nation. Loretta certainly wasn't the first woman to fall for a "danceable, romanceable man," as one journalist would later put it. Or as they say on *The Young and the Restless*: "Love is a mental illness."

Some of Loretta's friends cried foul right away. "That story is bullshit," one exclaimed. Skyla Petersen, who'd already been a friend for nearly fifteen years, remembers being there the day Taw arrived. "He was a smooth talker and very smart, but come on, he has no money, no luggage. I never understood where he got the motorcycle, but I'm sure he had a story all worked out about that, too. But Loretta bought it all. I couldn't believe it." Nevertheless, she acknowledges, love and logic have never been on speaking terms.

Loretta's four sisters couldn't believe it either, seeing red flags all over this story. Baby sister Darla Neal said there was such concern, she'd flown to Phoenix specifically to meet this new man in her sister's life. "I stayed with them for three days," Darla remembers. "I have a great bullshit detector, and his story didn't ring true. I went to Loretta and I told her all her sisters were very concerned. 'You don't know anything about this guy—he has no family, no friends.'"

She can still recite Loretta's response: "I know what I'm doing, and it's none of your business." Darla wishes now that she would have fought back, but "in our family, we're taught to keep the peace." So what could she say? She couldn't force her sister to throw him out, but in all the years to come, the sisters kept a close eye on Taw Benderly.

By the time Darla sounded the alarm, Loretta and Taw were already sharing a bedroom. And then they were sharing a life, and then they were sharing her bank account, because neither the lost paycheck nor the suitcase ever showed up. But he hadn't lied about being a gourmet cook, and he could fix anything, and he jumped right in to be helpful wherever he could. Besides, he was so incredibly charming—his deep, resonant voice was almost hypnotizing—that Loretta clung to the hope that all the rest of it would come true someday too. And so she opened her checkbook to all of Taw's promises.

He presented an impressive résumé filled with business degrees and work history, as well as detailed drawings of his inventions. He was constantly on the phone, setting up deals and making contacts, and he was regularly in meetings with potential "partners" for his ideas. Taw was taken with the incredible potential of solar power and thought he could help "educate" the world to all its uses. He had "big plans" to create a solar power plant on the island of Lanai that Scott would manage for him.

To prove he was on the up and up, Taw brought legitimate businessmen into their lives, like Gary Bailey from a North Carolina company called Duke Solar. Gary and his wife, Laura, became close friends of Loretta and Taw, and it was clear to Loretta that Gary was impressed with the brainpower that lived on Manhattan Drive in Tempe. "Taw was extremely bright and he had an amazing network of people in government and private business—he could open doors," Bailey remembers. But he, too, watched in amazement as Taw's ideas never went anywhere, including inventions Bailey thought could be a success. "Taw just oversold things," he says. "He was great at the knowledge, but didn't know how to close a deal. It was so sad to me."

Some of Loretta's money went for Taw's "solar car cover" invention. Some to his "serrated lawn mower blades." Some to his "transducer audio speakers." For years, she refused to admit that Taw's inventions were a money pit and one after another, each one failed to bring the riches he promised.

"I told my mother once I was tired of hearing about those inventions," Scott remembers. "I told her, 'They're old, outdated and they're stupid, stupid things. I've been hearing about the same three things for ten years now. Technology has moved on and the time has come for you to move on.' That worried me about her, that she was buying into it." How did Loretta react? "She took it and understood," he recalls.

Scott had recently told her he was moving on too, bowing out of the Lanai solar plant that never got out of the planning stage anyway, even though Taw and Loretta had taken dozens of trips to Denver where he supposedly was meeting with investors. In truth, Scott found, the investors never showed up and the trips were mainly visits with Loretta's sister, Shirley.

But Taw never once acted as though he were a failure. He kept asking for more and more support for the big payday that was always just around the corner. He hit up everyone who came into their circle to invest in his schemes. Loretta had invested heavily; so had her daughter, Terri; some of their friends were listed as official investors; neighbors, too. Not everyone saw the magic and potential fortune he was trying to sell, and onlookers always found it amazing that Taw had such a hostile attitude towards those who turned him down but no shame to those whose money he lost.

But Loretta was in a different boat. She either wouldn't or couldn't turn him down until there was nothing more to give. She kept praying that Taw's dreams had some substance. She needed for him to succeed as much as he did. She finally admitted to a girlfriend that by the time she doubted his stories—by the time she actually entertained the thought that he was lying to her—she had loaned him so much money, she needed to keep him around in hopes she'd get some of it back. She'd gambled everything on this man, and she needed him to make it so she could survive. Sometime over the years, she stopped romancing the idea of getting rich through him, and settled for the basic hope he'd help with the monthly expenses. But most months, even that was too much to hope for.

You couldn't see that from the outside, from the public face of this lovely home in this lovely neighborhood; not from the well-dressed and well-groomed couple who emerged from it, seemingly successful and secure.

No one could guess that for years Loretta had lain awake at night worrying about the bills and the collection notices. She scrimped and saved and watched every penny, because sometimes, by the end of the month, that was all that was left. No wonder the fear of financial insecurity dominated her outlook. So did her other fear, the one common to "women of a certain age"—Loretta Bowersock was convinced she was "too old to start over." She believed she'd "made her bed and must lie in it." She tried, as best she could, to make the most of it and see it through, and somewhere in the back of her mind, she must have believed that certainly *someday*, one of Taw's schemes would work out.

It hadn't always been that way, and the irony was that Loretta had done just fine alone. After her divorce, she'd supported herself and finished raising Terri on her own strength and her own skill. For some seventeen years before Taw showed up, she'd proven herself a capable and energetic businesswoman, first teaching tennis, then establishing a tennis club at San Marcos Golf Resort in Chandler. She opened a tennis pro shop and ran it for seven years. When it closed, it wasn't because she failed, but because the resort hadn't lived up to its promises. And her letters of recommendation came from among the leading citizens of Arizona, like grocery magnate and community activist Eddie Basha, who wrote in February of 1978:

> It is a privilege for me to write this letter of recommendation for Loretta Bowersock. I became acquainted with Loretta during the first part of 1974 on the occasion of her association with the San Marcos Resort. In my opinion, what she accomplished was nothing short of miraculous. . . . I heartily recommend Loretta Bowersock to you as both a tennis instructor and as a proprietor of a pro shop. She is a very talented woman and a very pleasant and friendly person to know.

Then in 1979, with her daughter, she opened a furniture consignment store named Terri's Consign & Design. Loretta was 44; Terri was 23. The business was growing—already two stores, many more to come—by the time Taw rode up on the hog in 1985.

By then, Loretta had bought her Manhattan Drive house in a town she loved. Tempe, Arizona, has lots of bragging rights: home to Arizona State University; home to a charming downtown that so reminds you of a quaint village; home to the Rio Salado Project that turned the normally dry Salt River into a lake that trains Olympic rowers. Unlike the other cities that make up the "Valley of the Sun"— Phoenix, Scottsdale, Glendale, Mesa—Tempe is hemmed in by other towns and an Indian reservation. Since it can't grow out, it has done the best with what it has, and many feel it has done some pretty wonderful things, even if politically, it is all over the board: not only did this area send the arch conservative Republican J. D. Hayworth to Congress, but Tempe kept electing an openly gay mayor, Democrat Neil Guiliano. Loretta had watched it all with a bent toward the Democratic side—she still had the Kerry–Edwards button she'd worn for months until the November 2004 election that sent George W. Bush back to the White House. One friend remembered Loretta wore the largest political button she'd ever seen, describing it as "the size of a dinner plate." And this very week Loretta had another reason to be proud of her town and her alma mater: Edward Prescott became the first ASU professor to win a Nobel Prize. He was honored for his work in economics. Saturday's paper would show him receiving the award the night before in Sweden from King Carl XVI Gustaf.

The consignment business had already doubled to four stores, and Loretta and Terri were starring in TV commercials. Life was pretty swell in the mid-1980s, in the days before Taw showed up. Loretta wanted a man in her life—that was like a constant toothache—but she had tons of friends and a very active social life.

And then this new man rode in and she thought she'd found her Prince Charming. She certainly treated him that way, bowing to his "superior intelligence," bending to his need for control, minding her *p*'s and *q*'s to make him happy. He almost immediately wanted to "help out" with Terri's Consign & Design, and Loretta insisted he join in. Yet he'd been nothing but a problem from the start, meddling with the finances and getting them in debt; constantly whispering to Loretta that Terri didn't know what she was doing; getting Loretta's ear and support until decisions that used to be made by mother and daughter were now being made by Taw. In 1987 he convinced Loretta to demand a buy-out from her daughter. Terri neither wanted nor could afford a buy-out at this point, but she agreed because it meant getting Taw out of her company. Terri couldn't afford to let him muck things up anymore, so she negotiated a monthly plan that paid her mother more than a quarter million dollars in today's money. The buy-out drove a wedge between mother and daughter—a wedge that would eventually become devastating—but Taw didn't seem to care how it hurt the women. His eye was always on Loretta's bottom line. It had to sting like hell that Terri went on, all on her own, to create a consignment empire that included thirty-six stores across the nation at one point, making the young woman a millionaire—but Taw had ideas how to cash in on that, too.

If Loretta had invested that buy-out windfall, she

could have secured her future. She'd eventually get an inheritance from her mother, too, that should have been a nice cushion. But all that money went down the rat hole of Taw's investments. As she'd later complain to girlfriends, money ran through his fingers like sand, and he could never get enough. He had no concept of saving for the future—his financial demands were now.

So by December 7, 2004, there was nothing left of the financial success Loretta had earned. Her certain income each month consisted of two sources: Social Security sent her $474, and her one big investment—a house on Abraham Lane in Phoenix that her daughter had bought for her years earlier—was rented for $1,495. She had such nice renters now, who always paid on time. Her own mortgage—the first she'd taken out thirty years ago, and second that had gone toward a failed Taw invention—cost her $1,209.08 a month. After she paid her mortgage, she had just $759.92 left for everything else. The only other income was the bits and pieces she and Taw earned from buying and selling items they picked up at yard and estate sales. They sold any furniture through her daughter's shop. The couple sometimes consigned estates themselves, taking a commission when they sold things, first through dealers and shops, and later, through eBay. Loretta had a real estate broker's license, but only sold a couple houses, so the big commissions from that never came through.

When things got desperate, she turned to Terri as a last resort. Her daughter was generous with loans and gifts, although the borrowing was humbling to proud

Loretta. She would have been devastated to know Taw often went begging for Terri's money, too. One of Terri's employees, Heather Dolan, remembers how the staff would whisper to one another on days when Taw would come to the corporate headquarters. "He'd sit in that lobby for hours on end until Terri would cut him a check," she says. "We thought it was so humiliating, but he didn't seem to mind."

"I always gave it to him because I didn't want Mother to be without," Terri says. "But I knew she'd be embarrassed if she knew he was borrowing from me, so most of the time, we kept it between us." Last year she'd slipped him $40,000. This year, it was $20,000. She didn't see herself as an "enabler," but resented every penny, for this was the man who'd come between her and her mother, and here she was, saving his butt time and again so he could look like a "big man" in her mother's eyes. She's sure he passed off her loans as though they were payments from investors on his worthless "inventions." And while her mother always promised that one day she'd repay the loans, Terri knew Taw had no intention of ever giving her back the tens of thousands she'd loaned him over the years.

Loretta had once written a demand letter to Taw—for a couple who lived together, they communicated surprisingly often by letters, most not very nice—insisting that he either contribute to the monthly bills or get out. It was an idle threat, repeated in later letters spread out years apart. At one point she demanded $6,000 a month as his share. She had to know she was dreaming.

So it was a delicious joy on Tuesday, December 7, 2004, when her investment house sold to those nice renters and they sent a wire transfer from Bank One for $69,119.25. And for once, Taw had helped maximize the windfall. He convinced her they would escape capital gains taxes if the money were wired into his business account so it would look like an investment fee. Loretta figured she'd be saving thousands. Now the money was safely wired to Technology Lab Inc., whose address was their Manhattan Drive home.

You can just imagine the big smile on her face that happy day. Loretta wouldn't live to see another Tuesday, but of course, she had no way of knowing that then.

Taw never had a payday, but this was a payday for Loretta. Now things could be different; now the constant anxieties could be over; now she could have the kind of life she'd so dreamed of. Besides, maybe now she could treat herself and fulfill some of the dreams she'd detailed nearly a year ago on a list she titled "What do I want for Christmas 2003–2004." It was both a practical and a fantasy list— from paying off credit cards to a three-to-five-day stay at a health spa; from gold pierced earrings and a "fashion statement purse" to a new entrance to the house: "front entry landscaped, including new sidewalk and driveway."

The number one thing on that Christmas list had been Loretta's big priority for so many years: "Better communication with Taw." You have to wonder if she snickered when she pulled the list out to review it, in light of her newfound financial bonanza. Getting through to Taw was a theme that had run through page after page of her personal journals. It was the focus of her self-improvement classes and the long, laborious inspections of her mind and her soul that she committed to paper, year after year.

In 1999 she wrote him:

I am no longer willing—indeed I was never willing— but I am no longer going to accept financial abuses, verbal abuses and shirking of your responsibilities.

But on November 10, 2001, while Taw was exiled to the guest room, she was writing to herself:

I have to set a deadline some time. I will not go this month without a financial contribution toward his expenses. Enough is Enough! He must get some money to operate, he cannot keep expecting me to support him and his business.

On December 10, 2002, she wrote:

Still no financial relief. Money withdrawn from personal and business accounts without entry in the checkbook. $17 left in the business account. $500 in sinking fund that he agreed was to avoid overdrawing account and bank charges—blatant disregard. Cannot control what he does with money. How do I protect myself against careless and unnecessary spending? Deceitful withdrawals from bank account? His willingness to "educate the world on energy" without receiving compensation? How do I protect myself from another lien being placed

*on my house? If bills are to be paid this month, he will
pay them. Either he can find a way or phones get turned
off. I don't want to be intimate and I know that there has
not been a change of attitude or skills to create a supportive relationship. I can't earn enough to pay the bills. I'm
through borrowing money to live on. It is very demeaning
to my self respect.*

In another letter, she warned:

*The only thing you can do to keep this relationship
from blowing up on a daily basis is create a steady, reli-
able, income that I can run a household in an organized,
predictable way. Until you do that, stop beating up on me
verbally for being unhappy about not having any money.*

And Taw gave back as good as he got. In a 1991
letter he mocked her complaints that "Taw, you have
brought too much baggage to our relationship," or
"Taw, you ruined my relationship with my daughter." He taunted that she should question her own
judgment if she were so unhappy and stayed with
him anyway.

In May of 2004, Taw spent several days working
on a Dr. Phil "Relationship Rescue" exercise. He
completed a series of sentences meant to get him to
see their problems:

WHAT MAKES ME ANGRY IS *feeling and being frustrated.*
WHEN I GET ANGRY I *use my voice to express it.*
I WOULD GIVE ANYTHING IF *my partner would be less
critical of small things.*

MY BEST QUALITY IS *my brain power.*
MY PARTNER HATES IT WHEN I *am not truthful.*
IT WOULD BE BEST *to be honest with Loretta.*
I CAN'T FORGIVE *myself for failure.*
I BELIEVE *in myself.*
WOMEN CERTAINLY *differ in how they view life and issues.*
WE NEVER SEEM TO *make the time to have mutual enjoyment.*
IT HURTS ME WHEN MY PARTNER *doesn't trust me, even though it is warranted.*

But while Taw clearly saw the problems—even admitting he wasn't trustworthy or truthful—the obvious solutions eluded him. There's no inkling he thought he needed to improve himself; instead, his partner needed to do the accommodating. His warnings to Loretta, when he fought back with his own harsh letters, were to dangle the possibility of walking out on her. He had to know this would terrify her.

But, of course, he never made a move to leave, and Loretta never made a move to throw him out. The best she could do was refuse to marry him because he offered no financial security. But she gave him so much control, that was just a technicality anyway. The threats and ultimatums were just talk, and all the self-help "rescues" in the world can't save a drowning person who won't grab for the safety rope. All this was simply scenes in their drama.

To Loretta, it was the great failing of her life. She tried to "forgive" herself for being weak and not standing firm, and not expecting more but accepting so little out of life. Somehow in all those classes and all those self-improvement seminars— all the hours of watching Dr. Phil on television— she never got the message that sometimes it's not *your* fault.

Forensic psychiatrist Dr. Steven Pitt, who'd look at all this later, says it isn't hard to see why this went on so long: "She wasn't hard-wired to deal with a guy so manipulative and cunning. She was an emotional hostage to this guy's manipulation."

But by this mild December day in 2004, with the wire transfer completed and a hefty nest egg in the bank, Loretta finally seemed done with her self-flagellation.

That day she wrote in her journal her first true words of freedom in eighteen years:

I will give him some money to get out of here and pay back Terri.

Was this day really the mark of a new beginning? Did she mean it this time? Was she going to buy him off and kick him out? Is that all it would take to get her life back—one more check and don't-let-the-screen-door-hit-you-in-the-ass? If she seriously entertained it, as her journal entry said, she'd have made an assessment, finding she was still fit, still pretty, still active. She'd taken good care of herself and she had that beautiful smile. Maybe it wasn't too late to start over, as scary as that was to someone who was looking at the last chapters of her life; maybe it wasn't so bad to be on your own—it certainly couldn't be worse than this.

She kept that joy with her for the next few days. On Wednesday, December 8, at 10:10 a.m., she had an appointment for a flu shot. The only other event in her day planner was for Saturday night dinner with her old friend, Lorraine Combs: "Combs. Dinner and Christmas lights."

Light tours are one of the happy holiday traditions in the Valley of the Sun, where it never snows and "White Christmas" is just an Irving Berlin song. Many don't even realize that the famous composer penned the Christmas classic while sitting around the pool at the Arizona Biltmore hotel in Phoenix one balmy December day in 1942.

So Valley families compensate for the very un-Christmas-y weather of 70- and 80-degree temperatures by decking out their homes with thousands of lights. Some go absolutely berserk over it—one set of brothers competes against each other to see who can be the most elaborate, and each of their yards is covered with up to 100,000 lights. It's the kind of thing you wouldn't believe if you didn't see it with your own eyes. And so many in Arizona spend a night making a light tour—limousine rentals are very big for this event in December—and the local papers print maps of holiday displays. Loretta had clipped one out to take on their after-dinner excursing.

It appears to have been a normal Saturday for Loretta and Taw. Their neighbor, Neil Crawford, remembers seeing Loretta cleaning out the double garage. She was always cleaning it or, as her journals show, nagging Taw to clean the messes he dumped there—often excess parts of his "inventions" that so cluttered the space, you could hardly get even one car inside. Loretta didn't like things messy, didn't like things out of place, and her journals show almost an obsession with getting the garage in order. In fact, one of her Christmas wishes the year before had been "clean garage by Jan. 15th to last for a year." Obviously, it was a resolution that didn't hold.

Another neighbor, Michelle Pazsoldan, was hanging her own Christmas lights when she saw Loretta sweeping the front porch while Taw tinkered in the garage on Saturday. Mrs. Pazsoldan considered Loretta and Taw "grandparent figures" to her little girls, and remembered they had recently given the toddlers a wicker tea set to play with. Her dominant memory of Taw is that he was "an eccentric."

Sometime Saturday, Loretta and Taw went into the Zales jewelry store in Fiesta Mall for what the clerk remembered as a strange visit. Police would summarize this account from clerk LaJean Sommerville:

The woman wanted one of her rings sized and needed it back before the end of the day. The man became angry when they were advised the ring could not be sized that quickly. The man said they needed the sizing done right away because they were leaving for Tucson in the morning. As the man became angry, the woman he was with became very meek and looked as if she were about to cry.

On Saturday afternoon, the couple went to a garage sale in the Arcadia area of Phoenix—not only a favorite hobby, but the way they supported themselves. After going through the housewares and trinkets and clothes, they had a rude awakening—Loretta's second vehicle, her 1991 white Dodge van, had broken down. They had it towed to their neighborhood Cobblestone Auto Spa to have the brakes fixed.

That afternoon, Loretta got an email she'd been expecting for at least a week. The subject line read "nonviolent communication." The message was from Carmen Falcon, who later explained that a week earlier, she and others had held a garage sale in Tempe to help raise scholarship money for people who wanted to take classes in non-violent communication. "The classes were only about seventy dollars for six weeks, but there were people already signed up who couldn't afford it and we knew there were others, too, so some of us got together and said we'd sell our old things to help out," Carmen remembers. One of the people who came to that sale was a "lovely woman" who was very interested in the classes. "We had a lovely conversation," Carmen remembers. "She was really excited about the classes and wanted to take them, but she didn't have the resources. I told her I'd email her the information, and I remember she was happy to get it. But we were so busy, it took me a couple days to send the information."

Carmen says she "never pays attention to the news," so was unaware what had happened to the "lovely woman." She was shocked to hear that Loretta had been murdered.

Carmen's email read:

*Here's the information you asked for at the garage
sale. She is a great teacher, the best for you.*

Then it gave the phone number for Christine Dove,
a clinical social worker who teaches and coaches people in non-violent communication through her Institute for Conscious Connections.

Loretta never called that number, and her name
rang no bells with Dove. "Most people interested in
non-violent communication aren't in life-threatening
situations," Dove says. "They want a deep connection with themselves and others. They want to know
how to authentically express themselves and empa-
thetically listen. They want to work it out and don't
want to stimulate a whole lot of reactivity in the other
person."

Christine Dove never knew Loretta Bowersock,
but she described her perfectly.

Loretta and Taw got home from the garage late
in the afternoon and they started cooking. Loretta set
the table with her best china. She was all smiles by the
time her guests arrived for dinner.

Lorraine Combs remembers that Saturday night
dinner as a "very, very pleasant evening" that also
included her daughter, Diane, and son, Bill. The dinner was a belated birthday party for Lorraine, whose
actual birthday had been in October when Loretta
and Taw were away. Taw gave her steak knives for a
birthday present.

"We ate in the dining room—china, silver, everything was exactly in the right place," Lorraine would
later say of the occasion. "Loretta served a roast."

She remembers a pleasant conversation covering what everyone was doing and their plans for the holidays. She would later tell police there wasn't any talk that night of Taw and Loretta taking any trips in the near future.

She and Loretta had been friends since 1971, when they met while standing in line to sign up for classes at Arizona State University. Lorraine remembers that the well-dressed woman in front of her turned around and asked what scent she was wearing. Lorraine was wearing Estée Lauder. That ice-breaker led to a friendship that included both professional and personal times together.

"We discovered we both loved bridge, and for years, every Sunday we played bridge. We spent a lot of time yakking on the phone. We became like a family," Lorraine remembers. It wasn't hard to like Loretta: "she had personality coming out of her ears and she was always willing to learn new things."

Like Loretta, Lorraine was divorced and a newcomer to Arizona. In Lorraine's case, she had stopped in Phoenix to see an old college roommate on her way from Iowa to a new life in California. She'll never forget that her horoscope that morning in the *Arizona Republic* said "an offer will be rescinded," and darned if the job she'd gone to California to accept wasn't withdrawn. She came back to Arizona and a friend got her involved in the Mesa YMCA, where she became program director. Lorraine hired Loretta to teach dance classes at the Y, and later they both taught tennis at the women's prison. For years, they'd take time during the summer to go sailing off Catalina in California, and Loretta and Taw were frequent visitors to Lorraine's summer cabin in Munds Park near Flagstaff. "I once got a Christmas card from Loretta saying, 'I spent more New Year's Eves with you than anyone I know,'" Lorraine says.

After dinner, Loretta took Lorraine into the spare bedroom to show her several of the gifts she'd already bought for Terri that Christmas—a table runner, green-and-red tablecloth, placemats, sock covers for her golf clubs. Lorraine was always so thankful they'd looked at the presents, because she was the only one left at Christmas to tell Terri these things were for her—the last gifts Loretta ever bought her daughter.

Then everyone climbed into Loretta's red Dodge Caravan—Taw drove, Loretta sat in the front, Lorraine and her adult children sat in back—and they drove all over looking at Christmas lights. In all, they spent about five hours together that night.

Lorraine's belated birthday dinner was the last social event on Loretta's calendar until the holidays. She had a lot to do, including more Christmas shopping. But her version wasn't the usual "run to the mall" adventure. Retail wasn't her favorite way to buy—second-hand was far more her style and her joy. Anyone can walk into a department store and find *something* for a gift—it takes real diligence and real determination to find the *perfect* memento for someone you love; it proves you've really been thinking about them and searching for them. On top of that, it's a delicious game to get that precisely-for-you present for little money. Loretta had learned long ago that it wasn't the amount you paid for something; it was the thoughtfulness and appropriateness of that gift.

Each year she'd have multiple gifts for her family and friends, and would delight in revealing how little she'd spent for each treasure. "How much do you think I paid for this?" was her favorite guessing game. She planned to play it again this year in her luscious living room. That was really the only important date noted on her Day-Timer: "Friday, December 24, Christmas Eve Dinner here."

On Sunday, December 12, Loretta would have curled up with the Sunday *Republic*, the biggest paper of the week, filled with stories and features and a fistful of ad supplements. There were some disturbing stories this day—the first report that Ukranian presidential candidate Viktor Yushchenko had been poisoned and disfigured with dioxin, and the picture that went with the article was absolutely awful, such a handsome face so ravished. There were hopeful stories, like the one on "Homebuyers Move In and Spend," bragging that one of every three dollars in Phoenix's $140 billion economy was generated by the housing industry. This was always the kind of news a Valley homeowner loved to hear— the best thing they ever did was invest in a house in this ever-growing state, where home values kept climbing up and up, and there was still no end in sight. Loretta was well aware that the Manhattan Drive house was her golden nest egg, and had increased in value tenfold since she'd first bought it. Like many in Arizona, her "financial portfolio" and her mortgage were one and the same. There wasn't much else, but there was a goldmine in a piece of real estate.

There also were funny things in the Sunday paper—especially if your sense of humor goes to the ironic. Scottsdale's famous Wild West theme park, Rawhide, had been sold to the Indians. It would join a thriving casino and a hotel and resort, and soon, a golf course. Anybody grounded in the history of Arizona had to find this the most delicious of paybacks—the Gila River tribe had once been successful farmers, until their water was cut off up stream for Anglo farms. They had faced great poverty until gambling came along and made the tribe rich. And now they were buying Arizona's premiere cowboy attraction. It was a perfect what-goes-around-comes-around, and Loretta would have relished the joke.

About 11:15 a.m., Lorraine called Loretta's cell phone and left a message, thanking her for the wonderful dinner. She never got a call back.

Terri stopped by for lunch—a sandwich and soup—and to complain that she wasn't feeling well. Maybe it was the flu that was going around. "We sat in the kitchen and had just an everyday conversation," she says now. "Taw kept stepping in and Mom said, 'Taw, we don't need you.' Geez, a mother and daughter couldn't even have a talk without him butting in. I don't even remember what we talked about, but probably something about weight and diet, because we were always talking about that. Mom was always giving me ideas on what to eat and how to take the weight off. She believed in natural foods and stuff like 'Don't drink the orange juice, eat the orange.' I felt the conversation was a little strained—it wasn't something you could see, you just got the feeling."

Her mother sent her home with chicken soup and a just-baked loaf of banana nut bread.

Scott called his mother that Sunday from Hawaii— one of his frequent weekly calls. They'd speak any- where from one to five times during any given week. "It was an ordinary conversation," he remembers, and about the only thing he could recall to police is that his mother reported her investment property had sold and she'd "made a profit of $40,000 to $60,000." He was happy for her, but mainly he re- members it as a usual family chat: What have you been doing? What's new? What's planned? It's the kind of Sunday call that happens with thousands of families across America every week. Scott doesn't remember thinking anything was amiss. He hung up believing things were pretty much same-ole-same- ole back in Tempe.

Loretta called her friend, Ursula Kramer, in Cali- fornia, but got her cell phone and left an upbeat mes- sage: "It's me. Let's talk. Got lots to tell." Ursula would remember she thought, "Oh wonderful—I knew her deal on the house had closed and she'd come into some money. And I thought, Oh great. Well, maybe things are going to start looking up and she's going to have some money, finally." Later Sun- day, a distraught Loretta called Joy Evans in California, a woman who considered herself Loretta's best friend.

"She asked if she could come over, and said, 'I'm really upset and I really need to talk to you.'" Joy pushed for details, but Loretta wouldn't say what had so riled her. Joy told her to come that very day, but Loretta said she needed to wait fourteen days to get a cheaper ticket.

Monday, December 13, started with a surprise—a pleasant surprise. It would be the last pleasant moment of Loretta Bowersock's life. "I don't know why, but for the second time in my life, I sent her flowers," Terri recalls. "I'm not a flower sender, but that day it just came in my heart that I wanted to show her I loved her." Loretta called her daughter at work to gush about the beautiful bouquet, but the call got dropped—Loretta's cell had a tendency to do that—and Terri remembers that she let it pass. "I was at work, so I just moved on." Terri spent the day with that special joy of daughters who have made their mothers happy.

But that was the only joy inside the house on Manhattan Drive that Monday. Today, Loretta was filled with the opposite emotions she'd had just a week ago. Sometime that day, everything in her world changed. There was no euphoria over her financial windfall. There was no feeling that this was a new beginning. There were no dreams of how to spend money, now that there was finally money to spend. There was more fear and more angst than anyone could bear, and Loretta's cell phone records show it.

At 3:33 p.m., she made the first of seventeen con-

secutive calls to ten different phone numbers at
Wells Fargo bank. The last call ended at 4:44 p.m.

   That one hour and eleven minutes on the phone
had to have constituted the most terrifying moments
of Loretta Bowersock's life.

CHAPTER 2

Getting Rid of Loretta

Loretta was dead by 6 p.m., Monday, December 13. No one will ever know for sure the exact moment of her death, but all indications are that it happened soon after her last phone call ended at 4:44. By about 6 p.m., Taw was calling her children with his cover story.

Loretta had dressed in a turtleneck sweater and slacks that day, going through her normal morning ritual that says a working woman gets dressed, puts on makeup, combs her hair and presents herself as though she were going to an office. It made no difference that the office in this case was the spare bedrooms down the hall, where Loretta and Taw each had their own desks. She would never have tolerated the normal attire for people who work at home, the casual clothes or even the bathrobe all day—Loretta felt that to be professional, you had to dress professional. Her only concession was to go barefoot in the comfort of her own home. On this day, she was probably wearing her beautiful diamond rings—the public display that she'd known success—because she always wore them, even for everyday.

It will always be a mystery what set off the chain of events that would end so horribly. Did Loretta intercept another letter from the bank—just like all the others Taw had so carefully kept out of her sight? Did she get a call that Taw had meant to grab first—just like the other calls he'd taken without sharing the news? Did some niggling suspicion make her snoop around on Taw's desk, where she found a threatening notice under a pile of papers? One of those things had to have happened, because until that afternoon, Loretta had no idea her world was falling apart, and that the man she'd pledged her life to for the last eighteen years was responsible.

The secret she uncovered that afternoon was shocking and shattering—so unbelievable it surely sent her into a rage—but it would remain a secret to everyone except these two for several more days.

At 3:33 p.m., she sat at the desk in her office and dialed the Wells Fargo office in Mesa, Arizona, for a call that lasted 24 seconds. Three minutes later, she called the Wells Fargo Home Mortgage office in nearby Gilbert and talked to someone for 66 seconds. At 3:38 p.m., she called the Phoenix office of Wells Fargo, but apparently didn't get through, for the call lasted only 6 seconds. Same for the next call, back to Mesa, which lasted 5 seconds. On retrying the Mesa number at 3:54 p.m., she talked for 33 seconds; then called back and talked another 34 seconds; then called Gilbert again for 31 seconds. The Scottsdale branch of Wells Fargo Home Mortgage was called at 3:59 p.m. for a 48-second call; Gilbert again, for 45 seconds; Phoenix again for 8; a redial to Phoenix created a call that lasted 76 seconds. At 4:15 p.m., she called the Gilbert office again for a 59-second call, then Phoenix again in two calls—

one for 10 seconds, the other for 50. At 4:20 p.m., she finally connected with someone who had answers for her anxious questions. She called the Wells Fargo 800-number and talked to someone for 404 seconds, or 6 minutes and 44 seconds. The next call was to Lonestar Mortgage at 4:29 p.m. lasting 109 seconds. And then the 800 number of Wells Fargo was dialed again and this final call lasted for 760 seconds, or 12 minutes. The call began at 4:32 p.m. and ended at 4:44.

Police would later discover, from inspecting Taw's computer, that for some of the time Loretta was receiving the astonishing news on the phone, he was at his desk in the next room, searching the Internet. So all the time she was watching her world shattering—hearing her safety net tearing—Taw was only a few feet away. He had to have known what was coming; had to have anticipated her fury. It's probably a given that he put into high gear his lie-out-of-anything talents; that he was making up excuses and answers to give Loretta when she confronted him. But even a guy like Taw Benderly eventually comes to the end of the line.

It is not hard to imagine the viciousness of their last battle. The few friends who had witnessed their confrontations in the past say their fights were nasty and direct. Loretta had a sharp tongue when she wanted to use it, and threw such direct broadsides that a lesser man than Taw would have buckled. He fought back with an air of supcriority, as though he were the smart, rational one and she was the hysteric, and his defense often included heavy doses of "You're to blame, too." Often, both sides had a legitimate beef.

But this time, Loretta's wrath couldn't be deflected by taking any blame on herself. This time she was totally the victim.

She probably hung up and screamed at him with full rage: "You liar. You thief. You son of a bitch. You loathsome asshole. How could you do this to us? How could you do this to me? After everything I've done for you. After all the sacrifices and all the loans and all the years? You steal from me? You lousy piece of crap. Get out! Right now, get out of my house!"

She probably threatened to call the cops and declared she'd be happy to see him behind bars as a common criminal. It's easy to hear her sneering that she didn't care what happened to him, that she was done with his worthless 66-year-old ass. It's safe to guess she bellowed that she was keeping every single thing they shared and he was on his way out with the clothes on his back. She likely cried as she screamed at him, and her friends say they can imagine her calling him every nasty name she could contrive.

Would she have made fun of his useless inventions and his constant schemes that always failed? Would she have told him the same secrets she wrote in her journal—that he was a know-it-all who usually was wrong; a boring egomaniac who wasn't any good in bed; a fool who her family laughed at behind his back?

Loretta wasn't a physically violent person, and she cherished her possessions, so she didn't smash vases or sweep items off the shelves in anger; or if she did, Taw eventually cleaned them up, because there was no sign of a struggle or violence in the house when police later checked.

But everyone who ever knew Loretta can imagine that savage scene. As her son, Scott, puts it, "I'm sure my mother went after his ass with a frying pan, but rather than get out of the house, and go to my sister's or the police, she went after him herself."

And no one who ever knew Taw imagines that he just stood there and took it. His ego was far too massive for that. His years of control—his entitlement of being in charge—would certainly not have disappeared at this moment, but would have kicked into overdrive. His humiliation would have triggered a level of rage he'd probably never felt before—it's a common finding as sociologists study human behavior. It's usual for them to find death row inmates telling how they killed as they were being degraded or shamed. Taw Benderly was a man who had to be right about everything—the complete dressing-down and the threats that Loretta was throwing around were far more than he could take.

"When she said 'Enough is enough,' he could not stand for that," says their long-time attorney, Michael St. George. "It would cause him to say, 'Nobody ever says that to *me*'!" St. George knew how angry Taw could become, having seen it himself over the years. "Every now and then he'd lose his temper, and it was a vicious loss," St. George remembers. "As cultured as he tried to be, it was a vicious thing to see." The attorney can see it happening as Loretta finally tried to throw Taw out, and that's one reason that the minute he heard Loretta was missing, "I knew he'd killed her."

Was Loretta facing Taw when he attacked for the last time, when he extinguished her life? Or was she sitting down, facing away from him and surprised at what came from behind?

Psychic after psychic would later tell her daughter that Loretta was probably standing and was hit hard over the head with a blunt instrument that didn't break the skin, and therefore, didn't leave any traces of blood inside the house. Most declared that Loretta had died almost instantly. For a long time, that was one of the few comforts Terri had—at least her mother hadn't suffered in those last seconds. Those who said they could "see" the murder saw Taw dragging her into the garage Loretta was always hoping to get cleaned up. They saw her laid on the floor near the water heater—the heater was such a strong image that some psychics thought her body was hidden inside it. Some psychics saw him wrapping the body in canvas or a sheet, before putting her into their red van, parked inside the closed garage.

It isn't easy to kill a person, even if you're a tall man and she's a short woman; even if you outweigh her by 150 pounds. There's the physical force it takes, always fighting against her struggle. There's an emotional toll, too, although that comes later. Police will tell you, a killer doesn't think about whose life is being snuffed out or why, he just thinks about getting the job done. Once a lethal attack is launched, he doesn't pause and wonder, "Maybe I shouldn't do this." Instead, experts say, a killer just thinks, "Let's get this over with." Only when it's done; only when there is no more struggling or clawing or breathing; only when the body has gone limp because there is no life left to hold it up—only then does the person who's become a killer come back to himself.

Did Taw sit down and cry over what he'd done? Did he ever hold Loretta and call her name and say how sorry he was? Or did he stalk around the house, ranting about the trouble *he* was now in; screaming at Loretta that this was all her fault and she'd driven him to it? No one will ever know. As more and more information about Taw and his personality emerged, people would make guesses—never kind ones—but nobody really knows how this man reacted when he realized he'd killed the woman who'd stuck with him longer than anyone in his entire life.

At 5 p.m., Taw drove the red van to his neighborhood Cobblestone Auto Spa to pick up the white van whose brakes were now fixed. He paid the $191.79 bill in cash—the station always demanded this longtime customer pay cash, manager Curtis Hecke would later tell police, even when Taw pleaded poverty. Hecke remembered that just the week before, Taw—he didn't know his last name—had tried to charge $601.41 in repairs on the same van's transmission, explaining that he was short on cash, but was getting money at the end of the month. Hecke wouldn't credit him, and Taw later came up with the full payment in cash.

Now the new bill was paid and Taw needed help getting his van home. He explained that he had come to the station alone because his "wife was home sick." He asked mechanic Alex Janicsek to follow him home so he could deliver one van and come back for the other. Janicsek took his own car to the

Manhattan Drive house. Taw parked the van in the driveway and got in Janicsek's car for the 10-minute ride back. The mechanic told police that Taw's demeanor had been "no different than usual, which was grumpy."

Was Loretta already dead, lying inside the garage, or did the fight happen once Taw got back home? Nobody knows, but it was all over by 6 p.m., because that's when Taw started his calls. The first was to Scott in Hawaii.

Scott and Taw had only seen each other a few times in all these years—Scott was seldom in Tempe, Loretta and Taw were never in Hawaii. But the two men had talked on the phone most weeks. Still, Scott found it "odd" that Taw would call just to chat. They weren't close, and Taw must have guessed that Scott held a low opinion of him. "He was a know-it-all, and pompous about it, and a bit of a turd," Scott says. "He knew everything down to how much food the cat should get—she couldn't even decide that. The only reason she was still with him was, she didn't want to be alone. But he seemed harmless."

However, Scott was in no mood this night to talk to the man who shared his mother's life. "It was an uninteresting conversation," Scott says now. "He dealt with watches that he sold on eBay, and he was asking what kind of watch I wanted. It was boring to me. I was trying to watch *The Amazing Race*, and he was talking about this boring stuff. He did sound a little weird, but I was distracted, trying to watch the show. I know now he was using the watches as a ploy, and this call was just to establish an alibi."

Scott told police that Taw had asked if he was depressed, and Scott told him he wasn't. "Benderly had nothing specific to speak of," police recounted from their phone interview with Scott. "Benderly did not mention Loretta in this conversation." But between 8 and 10 p.m., Tempe time, Scott got a second call from Benderly. This time, Benderly reported that he and Loretta were planning to go to Tucson to have a meeting at the University of Arizona the following day—a possible business deal. Scott, who had visited on the phone with his mother on Sunday, informed police that he didn't talk to her during either call, but had told Taw to have a good time in Tucson.

After the first call to Scott, Taw called Terri to tell her about the Tucson trip, saying that they'd be stopping there for a business meeting and then going on to Mexico for three or four days. Terri remembers that Taw twice told her over the phone how much her mother loved the flowers she'd sent that morning. Little could she guess that these would be the only funeral flowers Loretta would have for a very long time. Or that while he was gushing about the flowers on the phone, in reality he had thrown them across the garage floor, where they lay broken and scattered at that very moment.

Taw spent Monday night packing. How long it took him, no one will ever know. If he ate supper, if he slept, if he dreamed, will always be a secret. But it had to have taken him a couple of hours to amass the treasures he loaded into Loretta's red 1996 Dodge Caravan—virtually everything of value the couple had in their home: guns, pictures, computers, jewelry.

Taw loaded the back with almost all the clothes he owned, from his summer shirts to his winter sweaters. And he packed a bag for Loretta—after all, they were going on a trip to Mexico, right?

He had to have formulated some kind of plan by now because he was staging the van to cover the stories he'd told Scott and Terri. So of course, they'd have clothes for the trip, and Loretta would take her cosmetics and toiletries, and she wouldn't leave home without her diamond rings, and they both needed their passports. The items of value could be explained as merchandise to sell at flea markets. How would he explain the pick and shovel he stashed in the back? How about that he'd need them when he and Loretta dug up geodes—even though nobody remembers them ever digging geodes, and friends say neither of them was the type to get dirty?

He kept filling up the van, covering the long lump on the floor that held the body of Loretta Bowersock. Did he keep piling things in because he feared someone would see the body? Was this a way of burying her? Did he calculate that he'd need to sell all these things to support himself? The kind of cash these items could bring would go a long way in Mexico, where it's said that an American Social Security check that barely squeaks you by in Arizona can let you live like a king just across the border.

We do know he took a call on Loretta's cell phone at 7:15 p.m. from her sisters, Darla Neal of Kansas and Shirley Gates of Colorado. They were in New York on a Christmas-shopping trip. Darla remembers that Taw answered Loretta's phone and said she was at the mall shopping and would probably shut down the stores. The sisters thought it was strange that Loretta would be out at night without her cell phone. Loretta didn't go out alone at night because she had trouble seeing as a result of unsuccessful eye surgery.

Taw told the sisters that he and Loretta were going to Tucson the next day because "he was going to an energy summit and he didn't know what resort they'd be staying in yet," Darla told police. She remembers that the sisters weren't impressed, thinking the important-sounding summit "was more of his BS." The next morning, Darla remembered saying she was surprised Loretta didn't call back " 'cause she was usually very good about calling back. She was very faithful about it." Shirley surmised that Loretta had gotten in too late to call and "we kind of dismissed it," Darla told police.

Tuesday morning, Taw went into the driveway, as usual, to pick up the *Arizona Republic*. A neighbor was outside, too, and shouted, "How's Loretta?" "She has a scratchy throat," Taw yelled back as he returned to the house. If he took time to glance at the state's largest daily newspaper that morning, he couldn't have been happy to read the headlines. "Jury Votes Death," they screamed, reporting that Scott Peterson had gotten the death penalty in California for killing his wife and their unborn son. "Courthouse Crowd Cheers," read the subhead.

Peterson had dumped Laci's pregnant body in the ocean, thinking the fish would eat it and destroy any evidence, but it had washed up months later. The trial had been both salacious and sickening. He would pay with his life for killing that beautiful young mother-to-be and the baby son she'd wanted to name Conner.

"Valley Reacts to Death Sentence" read the head-line on an inside story. It began: "Although I am not a proponent of the death penalty, I would say that if there is any case that it was deserved, this was it," said Stephanie Orr, executive director of CASA, the Center for Prevention of Abuse and Violence. At the Sojourner Center, a domestic violence shelter since 1977, a resident said, "Hopefully it's opened up peo-ple's eyes to domestic violence somewhat. Hopefully they will keep going after the men that are abusive to women and they don't overlook it so easy."

The Peterson murder had occurred almost two years to the day of this verdict, decided after eleven and a half hours of deliberation over three days. The 32-year-old Peterson, a former fertilizer salesman with the good looks of a movie star, was now housed in San Quentin.

It's a good bet Taw read the story—his fascination with the Scott Peterson case in the days to come would border on a fixation.

Just before 9 a.m., Taw pushed the button for the automatic door opener and backed out of the garage. It appeared that he never intended to return to this address. There was nothing left in the house of real value, except things far too large to move, like the furniture.

He turned left when he came to McClintock Drive—named after a pioneer Arizona journalist who was one of Teddy Roosevelt's Rough Riders—and stopped to gas up at the Cobblestone Mobil sta-tion. He put the $17.48 on his Visa card at 9:05 a.m.

Twenty minutes later, he withdrew $24,000 cash from the Wells Fargo bank at Lakeshore Drive and Baseline Road. At 9:53 a.m., he purchased two new cell phones from the Sprint phone center on Southern Avenue, but the phones were never activated.

He took Highway 60 west, driving on one of the five lanes whose walls are decorated with Indian symbols. He was leaving behind the population center of Arizona—one of the most populous areas of the entire Southwest—with a capital that had just become the fifth largest city in the nation. He drove past the giant outlet mall called Arizona Mills, and followed the Tucson exit onto Interstate 10, which runs from Florida to California across the southern United States. Arizona's second largest city was 115 miles away.

Did he think of Terri when he passed Elliot Road, and all the times he'd taken this exit to her ritzy home in the Ahwatukee development that dominates the southern boundary of Phoenix? Did he notice the neon casino signs to Wild Horse Pass? Did he see the billboard that shouted a strange message at this particular moment: "It's a short drive to a luckier you"?

It's a safe bet that Taw Benderly was driving the speed limit this day—close to 75, but not much faster and not much slower. No sense drawing any attention. It's a given that he drove in the right-hand lane, since drivers in the left passing lane make it clear they think 75 is a naive suggestion on a long, boring road where 85 or 90 is a far more comfortable speed. Left-lane drivers get very nasty if folks try to assert their right to drive the speed limit in the "fast lane." Benderly wouldn't have created such a stir—not with the cargo he was carrying.

Was he looking for a turnoff every mile he drove, past the shrubs and palo verde trees? Did he already have his map, and had he studied it before he got behind the wheel? Did he notice when he crossed the bone-dry Gila River—recognizable only because of a bridge and a sign? By the time he got to the first rest area south of Phoenix—popular with tired truck drivers and families who need a potty break—the foothills were snuggling up to the highway, covered with their saguaros and chollas, and you have to wonder if they looked like good hiding places. He drove past the Florence exit, leading to Arizona's first prison, which still houses the death chamber. He watched the mountains fall away again from the highway, revealing clusters of trailers and a shabby house now and then.

At 10:15 a.m., he called Terri at her office, where she had a series of meetings planned for the day and was, as usual, extra-busy. He claimed they were still at home and her mother was out having a massage, but they were leaving for Tucson as soon as she returned. He reiterated that they would be back in about a week. Terri was impatient with the call— Why was he calling with such detail? This wasn't like him—and brushed him off with the perfunctory "Drive safely."

Just before 11 a.m. he took Exit 198—locally called Jimmie Kerr Boulevard after one of the area's favorite politicians who spent over 40 years of service to the folks here—to the Outlets at Casa Grande, a long strip of shops facing the freeway painted grey with teal blue trim and red tile roofs. There's a Pfaltzgraff and Gap Outlet, a Book Warehouse and Styles for Less, a Big Dogs and Kitchen Collection, a Sears and Reebok, a Liz Claiborne and an Amish Furniture Store and lots more. A giant American flag flies over it all, and most of the site is devoted to the gargantuan parking lot, softened now and then with fan palms, miniature oleanders and green-barbed palo verde trees.

At 11:04 a.m., Taw used his credit card to make a purchase at the mall. Certainly he should have known he was leaving a trail of crumbs behind him every time he used his credit card. It's a common enough plot in any thriller—someone on the run is nabbed because they naively used their card for much-needed cash or a ticket out of town. And police or the FBI, or sometimes the bad guys who have a computer hacker handy, monitor the card use in real time, and within a minute or two, the hapless fugitive is nabbed.

Taw Benderly loved thrillers, he loved mysteries, and he—the man who thought he knew just about everything about anything—had to know that a credit-card receipt is one of the most precise documents a person can create. Most people never look at the thin white slips they get in return for their signature on the dotted line, but one look can tell you why police find these documents so wonderful.

There's the name of the store, its city and state, and often its phone number. There's the name and identity number of the clerk who made the transaction. There's the date and time. There's the list of what was purchased, its price and the tax. There's the name of the credit card that was used and its last four identifying numbers. There's the name of the card-holder and the approval number for this transaction. Some cards have even more—if it's at a restaurant, it will show how many guests were served and some-times the name of the server. Yes, a credit card re-ceipt is a small novella of a moment of one's life, and in this case it would tell police that Taw Benderly had bought two baseball caps at Casa Grande at precisely 11:04 a.m. on Tuesday, December 14, 2004.

The next time he used his credit card—the next crumb in the trail—was two hours later at 1:10 p.m. In normal travel, by then he would have been shop-ping in the "Old Pueblo" of Tucson, Arizona. It had begun life in 1776 as a walled Spanish presidio, went on to be the temporary capital of the Arizona Terri-tory and now was the proud home of the University of Arizona. The outlet mall is only 65 miles north of Tucson on Interstate 10, and even when there's lots of road work, which there often is in Arizona, it only takes about an hour to drive the distance.

But Taw wasn't in Tucson at 1:10 p.m. when he next handed over the plastic. He was just five miles from the outlet mall that he'd reached by taking Exit 198. Now he'd taken Exit 200 to Love's Travel Stop. In 126 minutes, he had hopped just two short exits down the road.

What had he been doing in those two hours? If he'd spent all that time shopping at the outlet mall, he didn't find a single thing he wanted to purchase. Did he stop to have lunch? Unlikely, since his pur-chase at Love's was two sandwiches.

There's only one thing separating the mall and the

towering Love's sign that is so familiar to truckers. That one thing is Exit 199. That's the exit you take to Interstate 8. If you're going to Yuma, you've got a 176-mile drive ahead of you; if San Diego is your destination, you're looking at 353 miles.

It's a long, monotonous drive down this road, where you're often warned that you're in a "blowing dust area." This is raw open desert, with tons of saguaro cactus—the official Arizona state cactus that is only found in the lower Sonoran Desert. Standing tall, with "arms" that reach out in strange directions, these sentinels of the desert look like tall plant people. Some of this land has been irrigated to grow cotton, but mostly this is the land of scorpions and rattlesnakes—including the diamondbacks that give their name to Phoenix's baseball team—and roadrunners and dozens of species of birds who build their nests by picking holes in the porous saguaros. Some of this land is on the Ak-Chin Indian Community— the new owners of the Rawhide theme park—whose ancestors farmed here before the 1853 Gadsden Purchase that bought southern Arizona from Mexico for $10 million. There's not much more here now than there was then. Hardly any houses or trailers. There is a sign for Maricopa, a town several miles off this road, but that's about it. You better have a good book-on-tape on or a strong radio station, because there's nothing much along here to entertain you on the long drive to somewhere else.

Did Taw Benderly drive down Interstate 8 this day, using up that two hours to go somewhere and then double back?

It would be the obvious question asked by anyone

knowing this geography, like police detectives, but there was no answer to that question for two days.

All that was certain was that at 1:10 p.m., Taw had used his credit card to buy two lunches at Arby's and get $10.01 worth of gas at Love's Travel Stop. Then he continued on to Tucson, down the divided four-lane highway.

The mountains were only a backdrop as he went on his way, because here the landscape is just a large expanse of dry land. Mile on mile, the only man-made things are power lines, although everyone predicts that someday houses, shopping centers, gas stations and golf courses will fill every inch of this space as Arizona continues to be one of the nation's fastest growing states.

The drive from Phoenix to Tucson is one of the most boring in all of Arizona—a state where most drives from Phoenix have something beautiful to offer. No matter what direction you drive from Phoenix, you're climbing—Phoenix sits in a low basin at sea level, like a giant drain, while the rest of the state is nestled in mountains that cover the entire range of environments, from desert to plush plateaus covered with pines. Going north from Phoenix, there's almost an instant change into exciting, mountainous terrain. But not this road south to Tucson—ending up in a city some 2,370 feet above sea level. No, this isn't a route you take for a scenic view, it's a road you take to get from here to there. The only real life is found at any given exit, with its gas stations and trinket shops and McDonald's. Billboards along the way advertise everything from future home sites and RV parks to cheap cigarettes and car dealers.

The Santa Fe railroad tracks lie to the east of the freeway, and there's hope someday they will carry more than freight, giving passengers a reprieve from the mundane drive with a ride on the rails. But after years of dreaming, this still seems a long way off.

Then all of a sudden, there's an abrupt and dramatic change as the Inter reach the pecan farms with their thousands of lush, mature trees bordering each side of the road. Anyone who didn't believe water could bring the desert alive has only to see these farms to accept the truth. Taw had to have noticed. The change is so startling, the farms are impossible to miss.

And, of course, he couldn't have overlooked Picacho Peak—nobody can. Its awkward, towering point juts 3,374 feet into the sky and can be seen for miles. This would have been just one of the oldest—22 million years—and more unusual mountains in Arizona until it marked its place in history on April 15, 1862. In the only Civil War battle in Arizona, three union soldiers were killed in a ninety-minute battle here as Union soldiers from California attacked a Confederate scouting party. It was the kind of lore Taw would have had at his fingertips, and would have recited to any passenger as they passed the peak.

But if he told the Civil War story this day, he was speaking to an empty van.

More than likely, he wasn't thinking about a 142-year-old story that isn't even included in most books on the Civil War—he would have been thinking about the story he would tell when he got to Tucson and there was no Loretta.

Did he practice his story out loud, listening to how convincing it sounded as he used his best resonance and phrasing to dramatically report that he had no idea where his beloved Loretta had disappeared to? Did he run through the inventory in the back of the van and remind himself about the cover story for every item—especially the dirty pick and shovel? Did he refold the Arizona map as he drove, the one he'd marked up sometime in the last twenty-four hours? Did he smile smugly, knowing police could search this van until kingdom come and they wouldn't find anything that proved Loretta was dead?

Who knows where, but somewhere along this drive—maybe as he passed the Rooster Cogburn ostrich ranch where you can feed the birds or buy feather dusters and eggs—he convinced himself he didn't need to run.

Taw Benderly drove into Tucson believing he could get away with murder.

CHAPTER 3

The Early Years

Her death was a horror story, but Loretta's middle years were the kind of fairy tale that inspires TV movies.

She went from a dismal marriage to life on her own to a television commercial star, all the time supporting her rambunctious but difficult daughter in a risky business venture that turned out a winner.

They wrote the television commercials themselves, and you could tell. They had a down-home folksiness about them that was both charming and a little hokey. Here was a cute mother-daughter team that had bucked all the odds and gone from rags to riches in less than a decade. Their enthusiasm was catching, and they'd become one of Arizona's favorite success stories.

"Mother and I have pre-selected the highest quality of furniture, and priced it right for you," 29-year-old Terri sang into the camera when the commercials began running in mid-1980, wandering through a crowded showroom set up like a home. She had a perky personality, and the camera loved her. "You can trust my mom. She inspects all the furniture to be sure it's clean and priced right."

Then Mom came on, although 50-year-old Loretta

was so trim and fit she could have passed for a sister. It wasn't hard imagining her as the tennis pro she'd been before she joined her daughter in this new venture. "Remember, things move fast at Terri's," she'd caution, showing off a couch or dining room set. "Like this wall unit, new fifteen-hundred; Terri's price, five-fifty. Or this five-hundred-dollar oil painting from a model home; Terri's price, one ninety-eight."

They wore clothes that had obviously come from their own closets. Loretta was always in a stylish dress, usually belted, her hair fixed just so. Terri was often more casual, a pantsuit or culottes. They appeared separately and together, always smiling, always admiring the "gently used" furniture they never called second-hand.

Somewhere in the thirty-second spot, the theme song would run: "We sell it for you, you buy it like new, at Terri's Consignment Furniture." And their remarkable success would be highlighted: "Thanks to you and Mom, Terri's has expanded again from one warehouse in 1979 to six adjoining showrooms today," went one early spot. By then, this idea of consigning used furniture had so taken off, they could brag that Terri's was "the largest consignment store in the country."

Those original spots would always end with Terri gushing, "Thanks, Mom."

Loretta and Terri Bowersock had lots to be enthusiastic about; lots to be thankful for. They quickly became a popular and successful novelty—a mother-daughter team that had created a new kind of business: nobody had ever sold used furniture on television commercials before; nobody had ever used the old consignment system for such big items, and nobody had a more fascinating story about why this had all happened.

Because all the odds said that success would continue to elude Loretta as she met the half-century mark, and that Terri would never make a mark in any profession—certainly would never, ever end up a millionaire.

Terri's earliest school memories are red pen scrawls across her homework saying "Poor work" or "Lazy." Loretta feared that her only daughter might be retarded, but when she went looking for answers from teachers, she found none. "While other second-graders were starting to read, I was staring at the alphabet chart trying to figure out what the letters meant," Terri recalls. "By third grade, I was drowning in a sea of confusion. I kept making mistakes the others weren't making any longer. It seemed like all the other kids were learning and growing up, but I was stuck being dumb and still a baby."

Testing showed she had dyslexia, when letters are perceived out of place or backward. But the learning disability—shared by such luminaries as Albert Einstein, Thomas Edison and Walt Disney—was little understood and less corrected in the early 1960s when Terri was in elementary school. Even teachers who should have known better didn't, and one once told her she was "as dumb as a cue ball."

"What was I going to do with my new found label?" Terri asks in a book she later wrote about her life.

Was I stupid? I started to avoid, at all costs, reading and writing. When I came face-to-face with having to read out loud, I turned into the class clown, hoping to be kicked out to the hallway. Once out in the hall, I slinked down to the floor and let the tears flow. I wasn't a bad kid! I wasn't a trouble maker!

I hated spelling bees, never once passing my first turn. To pass a test, I had to cheat. I still remember my teacher yelling at me to "keep my eyes on my own paper, cheaters are bad." I had a choice to make right then and there, either turn my paper in with nothing on it and look totally stupid, or to get a lot better at cheating. I opted for cheating. If I hadn't, I'd be the oldest third grader in America. Despite my improved cheating abilities, I still flunked third grade. It became quite clear to me, I needed more survival skills.

Over the years, she developed a set of personal skills that helped her skate through school:

I learned that if the teacher liked me I had a better chance of passing—regardless of my grades. So I concentrated on getting them to like me.

Skill two: When other kids were making fun of me and calling me names, it was better to join in and make a joke, hiding my true feelings. As time went on, I even went a step further, and cut myself down first before anyone else could. I thought my emotions didn't count, buying into the concept that everyone was better than me.

Skill three: It was better to lay low and blend into the background. The less attention I drew to myself, the better. I stayed away from joining any clubs and never volunteered for any projects.

She also learned that her "dummy" status kept her locked in a low social set:

Cheerleaders, band members, yearbook members and newspaper staff clearly wanted nothing to do with a dummy. As a result, I developed low self-esteem and found myself accepted only by the "bad kids" who hung out across the street. Even then, I knew I wasn't really a bad kid. I didn't like to break rules and somehow I managed to be somewhere else when the real trouble happened. Unfortunately, that can't be said for everyone in groups such as mine. In fact, statistics show that 80 percent of children in the juvenile prison system are documented as learning disabled.

While her family enjoyed the "class clown" bravado that Terri developed as a survival mechanism, they weren't at all happy with the crowds she ran with, and her teenage years were marked with loud and awful fights with her mother. At one point, Terri ran away from home. The two clashed over everything a mother and rebellious teenage daughter can fight over—how Terri dressed, the amount of makeup she wore, how late she stayed out, who she went out with.

By the time Terri graduated from high school in 1975, she had only a third-grade reading level and fifth-grade math skills. She went through two years of community college, focusing on discussion groups, rather than writing and testing. She tried college, but lasted only two months at Arizona State University before it was clear she was out of her league.

"How was I going to get a job when I couldn't even fill out a job application?" she wondered. It was not only her worry, but Loretta's constant concern. By now, Loretta was divorced and her son was on his own. She was raising her difficult teenager alone, and in the back of her mind, she wondered if her "slow" daughter would ever be able to make an independent living.

Terri decided to start her own business to avoid the dreaded job applications, and established a lunch cart at a golf course where Loretta worked. Later, she managed the gift shop at a resort where Loretta was the tennis pro. But neither business created much income, and neither one fed an ego starved to overcome her handicap.

"I wanted to become 'somebody,'" she remembers in her book. "I needed to show my friends, family and teachers that I wasn't dumb; and I definitely wasn't lazy. I needed to prove myself and I needed to do it in a big way." Although she leaves her out of that list, Terri most wanted to make Loretta proud of her. While Loretta seemed to succeed at whatever she did, Terri was always struggling; while Loretta was always trim and fit, Terri was always fighting her weight; while Loretta was popular in the best circles, Terri was shut out of that crowd. So becoming "successful"—making Mom proud and feeling her love—became paramount to Terri.

The way to success presented itself on a trip to Kansas City to visit her father in 1979. "Dad took me to visit Betty, his friend who operated the Clearing House Consignment Shop out of a little house," she says. "There, I saw sterling silver, china, small furniture and knick-knacks for sale. People were actually having fun as they purchased what others no longer needed or wanted. Betty graciously explained how she managed the business. By the time the day was over, I knew I could do it. I knew I had the sales skills."

Instead of sleeping that night, she mapped out a business plan, and around midnight, called her mother back in Phoenix. "We're going to be rich!" she announced to a sleepy Loretta. "Oh, now what?" she remembers her mother asking before dismissing the idea of selling used furniture as being "too much like *Sanford and Son*," the popular television series about junk dealers. "Mom was as unenthusiastic as I was enthusiastic," Terri recalls.

On the flight home, Terri drew up her business plan, although it didn't resemble anything Donald Trump would recognize. "I created mine with crayons and colored pencils," Terri says. "Designing my success, I actually drew how the store would look. Although Mom wasn't totally convinced by my plan, my persuasiveness and determination to move forward convinced her."

As she'd always done, Mom promised to help, although she took on Terri's new project as a second job and continued as the tennis pro at a resort. Terri got the only loan she'd ever need for her new business—$2,000 from Grandma Gladys. "Climbing on my college-days motorcycle, I went to find a store location," Terri says. "I was so naive I didn't know there were real-estate people willing to do this legwork. I saw a 'For Lease' sign and went in to chat with the store owner. After agreeing to the monthly rent, I was handed the lease to sign. Unable to read the legal jargon, I faked reading it. Carefully, I guessed how long it would take to read a document that size. After waiting for that amount of time to pass, and not a moment longer, I eagerly signed my name. Presto! I was in business!"

She opened the store with her grandma's money, a rented pickup and two sets of old furniture: her childhood bedroom group and Loretta's old living room suite.

The first weeks weren't easy. The consignment concept had never been used for large furniture before, and people would walk into the shop and ask, "What is this place?" When they found out, some thought it a good way to get rid of their junk— merchandise far below the standards Terri and Loretta set. The stuff that did suit them had to be hauled— far too often from second-story apartments, Terri remembers—down to the borrowed truck and then to the store. She says that both she and her mom often went home at night with sore muscles, scraped knuckles and bruises.

The business was slowly catching on, and it soon became clear they needed their own truck. So they bought "Ol' Blue," a used blue pickup that has stayed in the business all these years.

The first store was along a busy street with a speed limit of 50 miles per hour, and Terri worried about how to slow traffic down enough for drivers to notice her merchandise. "So we put furniture on the curb and propped up a mannequin from Mom's tennis shop," she says. "Dressed in a short tennis skirt and one of Mom's wigs, the mannequin appeared to be happily waving at people driving by. Truck drivers even honked and whistled." One day a speeding truck upset the mannequin, throwing it into the street where both arms broke off. "Seizing the opportunity, I called the newspaper," Terri remembers. "There's been a mannequin accident" she shouted, and a laughing reporter soon showed up.

The funny story ran on the front page two days later, and Terri's consignment store had its first free publicity. "I'd finally found something I was good at," she proudly recalls in her book. "I—Terri, the dummy—had a talent for promotion, marketing and advertising."

That mannequin turned out to be a godsend for the new business. The *East Valley Tribune* ran a three-picture photo feature of Loretta with the doll on its local section page, while the *Arizona Republic* ran a photo of Loretta fixing its wig, with a caption that noted the mannequin was named "Loretta" because "the two look alike—when the dummy's wig is in place."

Terri and Loretta had a unique story to tell, and the Arizona media were glad to tell it. The *Republic* ran a glowing feature about their expanding business, noting that they had to work out their very different styles—and their roles as mother and daughter—to make it succeed. It ran with a picture of the two women beaming into the camera from a showroom filled with scrumptious furniture. Loretta is quoted as saying, "At first we realized we'd slip into the naughty-girl-and-the-mother-telling-her-what-to-do routine. We had to get it on an equal basis. Now it always comes down to a question of, 'Is this good for the business?' " Terri was quoted as saying: "It's ironic that she's now my best friend, my partner and mom. But this never would have survived with only one of us."

The story prompted Loretta's old friend Eddie Basha—himself a prominent and successful businessman—to send the kind of note that always brings a smile:

Hi Loretta: If you need a place to invest all that money you are making, please call! I could sure use the help. Congratulations on the fine article, I hope all continues well with you. Hi to Terri.

But the talent Terri didn't have—the ability to read—came back to haunt her. Eight months into the venture she discovered that the lease she'd signed for the first store was an illegal sublease. She was given thirty days to move or have the doors locked. "Everything I owned and everything that was consigned would be trapped inside," she notes. "Once again, I was on the street looking for a home for Terri's consignment store." But she had learned an important lesson: "It is cheaper to have a lawyer read legal documents before signing them than to pay the consequences." Unfortunately, it was a lesson that didn't stick when she needed it most, several years down the line.

This time she found a 3,000-square-foot space that allowed her to expand the business—but it wasn't on a busy street, so she needed a new "hook" to get publicity. If father-son businesses were such a big deal, why not mother-daughter businesses? she wondered, especially divorced mothers and their daughters in a state with one of the nation's highest divorce rates. It worked. The story, with a couple pictures, ran in the Sunday business section. "The next day, three hundred people, mostly mothers and daughters, came to the store," she says. "In addition to helping boost our monthly sales volume from $40,000 to $60,000, the article set off a series of stories in small neighborhood newspapers and several magazines."

The one part of the story she wasn't telling then was about her dyslexia—she was afraid people wouldn't trust a businesswoman who couldn't read.

The press coverage brought more business—both buyers and sellers. But the Bowersock women also discovered they didn't have to sit back and wait for folks or furniture to show up. They were naturals at furniture auctions—although an early experience was both painful and expensive: they bid against each other until the auctioneer noticed. "Boy, did we feel like amateurs," Terri says.

It was always important that the merchandise look as good as possible—that was a major selling point—but lining it up along the walls of the shop just didn't work. Then one day a friend who had design talent visited, and he suggested Terri set up the furniture as though it were in a home. He came by "like a fairy godfather" and helped her redesign the store so it was in "room" groupings. "Furniture began selling faster in complete room settings with our new look," she says.

But with more sales came more auctions and more collecting furniture, and it was all getting to be too much for one full-time Terri and one part-time Loretta. "How could I convince her to leave the tennis business and work with me full-time?" Terri wondered. "I pointed out Arizona's high rate of skin cancer. It worked. I convinced her to give up teaching tennis and take up the consignment business full-time."

The growing success also launched them in a new direction: interior designers discovered the quality of their merchandise and became regular customers. "Mom began to order some new items, so that we could consistently provide both the new and 'gently used' furnishings that designers wanted," Terri says. "Proud of the new concept we created, Terri's Consignment Furniture then became Terri's Consign and Design. Thanks to Mom, we were no longer 'Sanford and Son.' "

When Terri first thought of television commercials, Loretta vetoed the idea as "too expensive." "No one had ever seen a television commercial for used furniture," Terri wrote.

Used cars, yes, but not furniture. Determined to be the first consignment store to advertise on television, I secretly saved the money needed and arranged for a production crew—without telling Mom until the day before the filming. As the cameramen tried to shoot the commercial, Mom frantically scurried around dusting the store. At the end of the spot, he told her to hand me the feather duster. "Thanks, Mom," I sarcastically replied, like any typical daughter. "Thanks, Mom," became the signoff of many TV commercials to come over the next ten years. Those two words established us as a mother-daughter business to the moms, step-moms and grandmothers who make the majority of furniture purchases. For years, mothers visiting the store would pinch my cheeks and say, "What a sweet daughter you are." Boy, did I have rosy cheeks! But our bank account was doubling, so I didn't mind.

The mother-daughter team worked side-by-side every day for eight years. But eventually, the business wore Loretta out, Terri writes, presenting the "public story" the two women would tell for so many years:

Knowing I could not stand in her way, I bought out Mom's half-interest in the business. As she went on to pursue a less physically demanding job of selling real estate, I pursued my dream of building the nationwide chain of stores I'd drawn in my colored-pencil business plan.

As the business prospered into the early 1990s, Terri became more and more comfortable with acknowledging her dyslexia. She eventually worked one-on-one with a teacher to create a visual mapping method for spelling. It took her reading level from the third grade to the college level:

Armed with my improved skills, I opened four Terri's Consign & Design stores during the next three years. Now I needed another public relations story to spread the word and keep growing. It was at this time that former First Lady Barbara Bush was starting the Literacy Volunteer

*Program. (One of her sons also happens to be dyslexic.)
Breaking with my tradition of hiding my dyslexia, I once
again called the reporters. Only this time, it was television news reporters.*

She spoke out about her learning disability and
how she'd overcome it—appearing on all the newscasts that day—and became one of the leading
voices on dyslexia, not only in Arizona, but in the
country.

Her book continues:

*From that exposure, the United States Chamber of Com-
merce and Connecticut Mutual Life Insurance nominated
me for the Blue Chip Award, given to small businesses for
their resourcefulness, resilience and determination. In a
matter of weeks, my story was being told in national magazines.*

As she started talking about the ailment that had
plagued her and then driven her to create her own
company, she found she had a knack for public
speaking.

*I started speaking for free at schools and prisons, for
women's groups, Rotary clubs—you name it. I knew that
the experience was helping me build confidence to speak
professionally.*

And she found she had a powerful message. Many
famous people had suffered from dyslexia, but it
hadn't held them back, just as it wasn't holding her
back. She stressed that dyslexia was a "challenge"

that had "nothing to do with intelligence," and would cite the evidence of dyslexic people known and respected in a variety of fields: writers Virginia Woolf, Agatha Christie and F. Scott Fitzgerald; actresses Whoopi Goldberg and Loretta Young; Olympic decathlon medalist Bruce Jenner, athlete Magic Johnson, comedian Jay Leno, aviator Charles Lindbergh, Generals George Patton and William Westmoreland, artist Leonardo da Vinci, actor Robin Williams and Presidents Dwight Eisenhower, Gerald Ford and John F. Kennedy.

Her new notoriety also helped her expand the company into franchising, which flourished into a sixteen-store empire coast to coast with $36 million in annual sales. And she topped it all off by writing her book: *Success: It Can Be Yours*, subtitled *How to be a Millionaire by Using Your Determination*. She dedicated the book "To people like myself who have learning disabilities."

And through it all, she always credited her mother. In her book, she gives an "extra special thanks" to Loretta:

> *You not only guided me as a child, but went above and beyond when you stuck with me as an adult and helped me find a way to support myself.*

Her mother's support also got credit as her national awards piled up: *Inc.* magazine's 1992 Retail Entrepreneur of the Year; *Inc.*'s 1994 Socially Responsible Entrepreneur Award; Avon's Woman of Enterprise Award in 1998, and *Entrepreneur* magazine's Woman of the Year. At home in Arizona, Terri repeatedly was named the state's number one woman business owner.

Terri Bowersock was the kind of success story a Western state like Arizona loves—self-made, appreciative, giving-back and still as common as an old shoe. And through it all, she was the dutiful, grateful daughter who knew her mother had helped make it all possible.

To all the world, these two were an enviable mother-daughter team most can only dream about. And they kept that image up, even when it fell apart and turned ugly.

Nowhere in her book does Terri Bowersock acknowledge that she had long ago stopped feeling like "Thanks, Mom," or that mother and daughter had barely spoken since 1991. Nor does she ever admit that Taw—whose picture is included in the book and is referred to as her stepfather—was the driving wedge that broke them apart.

Certainly no one knew that at Terri's grand moment of triumph—her appearance on *The Oprah Winfrey Show* on April 29, 1998—she snubbed her mother.

Terri can still recite all the details of the day she got the call asking her to be on *Oprah*. She was at her office, they were having a meeting, her secretary puts through a call, even though Terri asked for them to be held. She was kind of impatient when she answered, then had to shush everyone when she heard the magic words, "I'm calling for *Oprah*." For almost anyone in this country, that's like a dream come true. To anyone, it's the ultimate sign of celebrity, of making it, of being a success. Not only is the show one of the most popular the nation has ever seen, but actually getting to meet Oprah—one of the most admired women on the planet—is breathtaking. Loretta was a huge fan of the show—that's how she first got to know about Dr. Phil, whose show also became a must-see on her television watching list. Terri knew her mother loved *Oprah*, but the day she got the call at her corporate office, they were embroiled in a legal fight, and weren't even talking. "I know it's sad, and that was the one thing she wanted to do, but I didn't take my mom to Chicago for the show," Terri admits. "I took my aunt Darla." It was her aunt who got to ride in the limousine and have breakfast at the fancy hotel and watch the makeup artist turn Terri into a glamour-puss. It was her aunt who got to sit in the audience as Oprah spun her magic in front of the cameras. It was her aunt front and center as Terri told her life story and Oprah marveled at how she'd overcome her learning disability to earn national awards. Loretta watched the show at home like everyone else. She had to have felt the slap in the face.

The show was pre-taped, and the day it ran, Terri was back in Phoenix appearing on Channel 3 newscasts to recount her grand adventure. On *Good Morning Arizona*, she told Tara Hitchcock that she'd attracted Oprah's attention because she'd won the Avon Award by turning her disadvantage of dyslexia into an opportunity. She shared the green-room experience with other guests of the day, including Hillary Clinton and Colin Powell. "In high school I was voted the least likely to succeed," she told Tara, while now she ran a company that earned $15 million worth of business. Any mementos from being on the nation's number one show? Tara asked. "I came away with a hat, a T-shirt and a coffee mug," Terri laughed.

At noon that day, she was interviewed by anchor Scott Passmore on how *Oprah* had spotlighted her life as part of a series on "rags to riches." It showed a clip of Oprah saying, "Terri says anyone can become a millionaire." Did you get much time with the television star? Passmore asked. No, Terri, said, "but I checked out her chair—I was checking out the furniture on her set, and it looks so big on television, but it really isn't."

Neither interviewer asked her about her co-founder and mother. No, at the moment this mother and daughter should have been reveling in the spotlight, there was a wall between them. The love Terri got back from her *Oprah* appearance came from strangers moved by her story. "You have given me hope," one 34-year-old dyslexic wrote her after the show. "I think maybe I can even learn to read better and maybe start a business myself." A mother of a 10-year-old with the learning disability wrote, "He goes through everything you described. It's all because not enough people understand about this problem. Maybe with you helping more people will understand dyslexia and we can find ways to help kids with it."

Nor was Loretta invited to many of the awards banquets that honored Terri for her business and personal accomplishments. "I'd take my friends with me," she remembers. "At one of those dinners, I realized I'd lost the joy of winning awards. I'd made myself numb because of the problems with my mother and I realized I'd only wanted to win awards to show off for her—to make her proud of me. But now I was so angry at her, that didn't matter anymore. And the awards didn't mean much anymore."

One of the reasons the bitterness went so deep is that Terri spent most of the 1990s in terrible pain, and it was her friends, not her mother, who helped her through that. She recalls that in 1992, she was approached by a "doctor" who claimed he had a cure for dyslexia. He said manipulating a bone in her mouth would cure the disability, and Terri jumped at the chance. She remembers a "horrible cracking" as he tried to move the bone, and her head started ringing. It rang, and left her in excruciating pain, for the next six years.

"One doctor told me, 'You are worse than people who have gone through serious car accidents,'" Terri remembers. She visited over 200 people, from doctors, to the Mayo Clinic, to psychics, natural healers and Indian medicine men, before she finally met a woman who helped get everything back in place and the pain stopped. And through all that, she and her mother were battling it out through lawyers. She remembers that one of the few times she spoke to her mother during those days was when Loretta showed up asking for a loan. "You asked for the money before you asked how I was," she told her mother as she threw a check at her.

That was the chapter of their life that Terri hoped no one would ever know—and if her mother had not been murdered, she would have probably kept that secret private forever. The daily press never uncovered the other story here, as they blanketed the airwaves and newspaper pages with stories about the missing Loretta. It wasn't until she sat down for gut-wrenching interviews with *Phoenix* magazine months after her mother's disappearance, that she came clean about the rift.

"But we had worked through it," Terri says with pain. "Things were so much better, and we were getting back to the old days and we were starting to have fun together, again. It was just beginning again."

The trip to Alaska had been a kick. Terri covered the cost for the week-long trip, which included Loretta, Taw and Deanna Jordon. "It was the first time I saw the old Loretta back—she just let go and had fun. It was like she said, 'I'm free,' and she got to be herself."

Deanna, who'd only known Loretta and Taw a couple of years, once remarked to Terri how different her mother seemed on this trip. "Now you're seeing my real mom," Terri said.

Loretta was busy every day. She'd have a facial, or do yoga; she always took a swim. "Taw wouldn't go, but the women went dancing—Mom danced with the instructor," Terri remembers. "We played Trivial Pursuit and Taw always thought he was the intelligent one, but Deanna was outdoing him, and you could see Mom was delighted Taw was getting beat."

At night, of course, they dressed for dinner and Loretta was the usual fashion plate. Terri and her mother came home with such fond memories. This was truly a new start, a new chapter. The old hurts were folded and put away, and now it was time to create happy new moments. Terri had that adorable picture of Loretta and Taw from the cruise. She was going to get it developed and have a copy made for them as soon as she had time.

And then time ran out. And as she handed out that picture to the media to use with their stories on her vanished mother, she still couldn't believe this nightmare was happening.

CHAPTER 4

Your Mother's Missing

December 14, 2004 was a lousy day for Terri Bowersock. She had back-to-back meetings all day, even had lunch brought in so as not to waste a minute. At 4.33 p.m., her secretary interrupted yet another meeting, saying Taw was calling from Tucson and something was wrong.

She took the call, listening with concern but not alarm as he told her Loretta wasn't anywhere to be found. He said that at 2 p.m., he'd dropped her off in Tucson at Dillard's in the Park Place mall—they were having a 75 percent off sale—and was supposed to pick her up at 4 p.m., but he couldn't find her. He wanted Terri to know, because this wasn't like her mother.

Terri thought at first he was only being impatient, that her mother was still shopping and just hadn't made the rendezvous. Taw said he was going to search the two-story shopping center and he'd call afterwards. By 5:30 p.m., he was back on the phone, reporting that he'd searched the center and Loretta was still missing.

Now Terri was alarmed—"Oh my God, had somebody kidnapped my mother, and what terrible things were they doing to her?" She asked her friend, Dee, to join her and jumped into her Porsche, making the normal two-hour trip to Tucson in an hour and fifteen minutes. On the way, she called her father, Dave, and his wife, Nancy, who lived in Tucson. They met Terri at Dillard's, where they made their own quick search before talking to police.

Although police didn't let on, by now they were already suspicious that this could be much more than a missing persons report.

Taw had called 911 at 5:43 p.m. "We have a woman that's been—my wife—that's been missing for an hour and forty-five minutes," he told the operator. "I was to pick her up at four. I was here at four and she did not show up, which is not like her. And we're not from Tucson." He reported that he'd talked with store security and mall security and would have talked to the city police patrolling the mall, except they were busy with something else. The operator interrupted, asking him to describe his wife, hearing back that she was a 69-year-old white female with pure silver hair. "She's wearing a gray outfit. She is wearing . . . wool gabardine slacks. She's wearing a gray ribbed turtleneck sweater, lightweight sweater. A waist-length gray jacket. And gray, um, suede shoes. So she's all in gray. But her hair is pure silver, it's not just white or gray."

He told the operator that he and the Dillard's security force had been searching. "They've been looking, we've paged, we've, um, Dillard's is the only store she shops in that's in this mall. You know, this is the first time she's been in this store, so — but we've been everywhere in the store. . . . They checked the restrooms, they checked the changing rooms. They've done substantial due diligence." He promised to wait at the south entrance for police to arrive.

In the meantime, the 911 operator called the emergency room of El Dorado Hospital to see if a 69-year-old white female by the name of Loretta Bowersock had been checked in. Negative.

Police arrived and questioned Taw briefly at the store, then took him back to the hotel room for a longer talk. Right away they noticed something that put them on alert. A police report later pointed out:

It was noted that Benderly had fresh scratches on his hand which appeared consistent with having a struggle and having several fingers scratch the hand.

Taw told police this story: Loretta had gone to a massage school that morning for a student massage—he couldn't remember the name of the school, but she went there often for her osteoporosis, and paid $20. They'd then left for Tucson about 10:30 a.m. Their first stop was at Love's, arriving between 11:30 and 11:40 a.m. He noted the traffic had been heavy. He said he'd bought gas there, and two roast beef sandwiches, which they'd eaten in the car as they drove, with bottled water to drink. He said he and Loretta had then stopped at a discount mall, where he'd bought two different baseball hats at two different stores. Loretta, meanwhile, had gone into a housewares store on her own. He said Loretta had been wearing jeans, a broad-stripe turtleneck sweater and a wine-colored jacket. He'd been wear-ing a dark blue, short-sleeved shirt, a blue windbreaker and cordovan loafers. They'd arrived in Tucson about 12:30, and checked into room 1613 of the Residence Inn. Taw had taken care of arranging the room while Loretta waited in the van. They'd gone to their room for about forty minutes while Loretta changed from her traveling clothes into the gray outfit she wore to the mall. She was carrying a gray clutch purse that contained her wallet, checks, a bank card and Dillard's credit card—Dillard's being the only department store she liked to shop in. He noted that both he and Loretta have cell phones, but "she carries it only fifty percent of the time, when I prompt her." He didn't think she'd taken it with her on this shopping trip. He said he'd gone back to the hotel to do some work for his upcoming meeting, which was yet to be arranged, and then left to pick up Loretta at the agreed-upon time of 4 p.m. He said he'd parked and waited twenty-four minutes for Loretta to come out. He'd checked his watch and noticed a stream of patrons coming out of Dillard's. He said he'd moved his car to another spot, then gone inside Dillard's to look for Loretta. When he couldn't find her, he'd gone to the customer service desk and reported her missing.

All this time, Terri was speeding to Tucson. She drove straight to the shopping mall, fighting off images that her mother was being molested or beaten by strangers. After talking with police at Dillard's and confirming that Loretta had still not been found, she rushed to the Residence Inn on Speedway Boulevard, where she found Taw and the police in room 1613.

Terri remembers she couldn't believe how calm and blasé Taw was. "I was the only one flipping out," she says. "I was expecting him to be shouting, 'Let's get out there and search for her,' but he wasn't."

Terri was anything but calm and blasé. She rushed around the room, fiddling with her cell phone— "We've got to call the media; we've got to make up flyers." All the time, she remembers, Taw was on the bed toying with his laptop. She thinks now he was systematically erasing files. She asked him if he had a picture of Loretta on his laptop and he did. She copied it onto a disc and used that picture to make up a "missing person" poster she had printed later that night at Kinko's. She called her friends in the Tucson media to tell them what was going on, and they promised to follow up. She emailed a picture of her mother to Tucson's Channel 4.

Taw picked up his cell phone to call Scott in Hawaii. Scott will never forget that call. "I hate rhetorical questions and rhetorical greetings, like 'How are you?' Because no one really cares," he says. "And of course, that's how Taw started." Imitating Taw's deep, measured voice, Scott says the call went like this:

TAW: *Hello, Scott, how are you?*
SCOTT: *Fine.*
TAW: *Your mother is missing.*
SCOTT: *Well, does she have her cell phone?*
TAW: *She refused to take it with her.*
SCOTT: *She will from now on!*
TAW: *I guess they got her.*

Then Taw handed the phone over to Terri, who told her brother Taw was reporting that a "suspi-

cious-looking van" had followed them earlier in the
day, and he was afraid they had kidnapped Loretta.
She promised to keep him informed.

Meanwhile, police were trying to calm Terri
down, suggesting what she thought was a worthless
gesture—they wanted her to search the suitcases to
see if there was anything missing, or any clues. How
this would help find her missing mom, Terri couldn't
understand, but the police were firm and so she went
into the changing area of the suite to look at her
mother's suitcase.

In her own journal, Terri would later write:

*6 suitcases, 5 filled with lots and lots of Taw's
clothes. One small suitcase of hers filled with 4 pants,
4 shirts, 4 underwears, 1 pair of shoes, no coat, and
makeup just thrown in a bag, like a handful just tossed
in. It was wrong, not how my mother would have
packed her bag. He said she was wearing a silver
turtleneck, with Jeans and gold jewelry, specifically
her favorite gold ring she wore all the time. Wrong.
She would never wear gold with silver. I felt a big lump
in my throat, I began to hide the fear that was in
my mind.*

It takes no expert in human behavior to realize that
a fastidious woman who took such pride in her appearance had never packed that bag for a trip of a week or
so. Just the number of underpants is enough to tell you
that, for a woman would want a fresh pair every day.

And whoever heard of a man taking five suitcases
for himself for a week's trip. Most married men rely

on their wives to pack for them in the first place. ("Did you bring my suit jacket? . . . Where's my razor? . . . Are there extra socks?") Even if Taw wasn't that kind of man, he had packed enough pants, shirts, sweaters and jackets to outfit a small men's store.

There was one small bag Taw said also belonged to Loretta, and when Terri started going through its contents, her first response was "Oh shit." She found all her mother's valuable rings inside. There was the large gold nugget–style ring with diamonds. There was the gold ring with rows of small diamonds. There was the "tiger eye" ring. "She always—always—wore her rings, and there they were," Terri remembers. "It just goes right through you."

But she forced herself to stay calm and didn't raise a fuss, because she now suspected that Taw had done something to her mother, and he was the only one who knew where she was. "You keep your enemies close," she explains. "Besides, he was my best resource."

Police asked to search Taw's van and he gave them permission, though he warned them that he had several valuable things inside and wanted to be sure they stayed safe. Police eventually had the van towed to their impound lot so they could do a more thorough, but secure, search.

Terri left with the police. Taw said he wanted to stay at the hotel and rest. "He said he had a sore back," Terri remembers, having no idea how he could have so strained his back. "I told the police the packing was all wrong, the makeup wasn't right, the rings shouldn't be there," she says. They told her

Taw's demeanor was inappropriate for an innocent man. She shared what she knew of their life—Taw was a control freak who always had these pie-in-the-sky ideas that never panned out, so, unknown to Loretta, he was constantly borrowing money from Terri. But he was also charming and certainly wasn't violent, and over the years, they'd seemed to make it work. They actually seemed to be OK, Terri concluded.

She got the copies of her mother's picture made. About 10 p.m., Dave, Nancy and Dee went back to Dillard's to pass them out, in case anyone there had seen Loretta that day.

Tucson homicide detective Fabian Pacheco didn't realize when he responded to the Bowersock report the next day that he was entering a case that would haunt him. By now the third-generation Arizonan, who'd grown up in nearby Nogales, had already investigated dozens of murders. "But this was probably the one case that stands out in my three years in homicide," he says. "It remained with me when I was promoted and left homicide to become a hostage negotiator." He still has Loretta's "Missing Person" poster—the same one he kept taped on the wall by his desk for more than a year.

By the time Taw Benderly came down to police headquarters for a formal interview in the late afternoon on Wednesday, December 15, Detective Pacheco was already sure he was looking at a murderer.

Tucson police had been very busy in the last twenty-four hours, because if Loretta really had been kidnapped, those first hours were the best period of time to search for her. Already, police had gone through the Dillard's security tapes. They began looking at the recordings from around 2 p.m., when Loretta had supposedly been dropped off, and they didn't like what they saw. They checked the charge receipts for that day and found none for Loretta Bowersock. They looked at the tapes from around the time Benderly had come looking for her, and what they found was very suspicious.

Routine checks were already tracking down credit card records, and Tucson had alerted Tempe that one of its citizens had gone missing. By chance, Tucson homicide detectives Bill Hanson and Roxanne Washington were in Phoenix that day on another case, and they went to the house on Manhattan Drive. Benderly had given police permission to search the house in case it would provide any clues on Loretta's whereabouts. What the officers found there sure didn't look good. They shared their findings with Tempe police, who went to court to get a formal search warrant. By 10:03 p.m. that night, a judge had issued the warrant and Tempe officers were going through the house inch by inch.

Pacheco had been getting reports all day, so he and his partner were well aware what evidence had turned up when they sat down with video equipment to tape the formal police interview with Benderly. To this day, he says it's amazing to watch that tape and notice how calm and self-assured Taw Benderly is. He sits there, sounding so educated and sophisticated, weaving a story filled with inconsistencies that prove he's lying: four, five, six points that nail him.

Police can usually spot a liar pretty quickly—folks

who have done something wrong are usually nervous and scared, and besides, most people aren't convincing liars under the best of circumstances. And when they spot one who lies again and again—lies that can be proven in court against official records like timed credit card receipts and computerized hotel check-ins—it's like a cat-and-mouse game. And the mouse is going to lose.

Tucson police were double-teaming the interview with Taw, with both Pacheco and Detective Jim Filippelli in the room. While Detective Filippelli started, Pacheco got Taw a bottle of water. It was 5 p.m. on Wednesday, December 15.

"We began the interview soft," Detective Pacheco remembers. "We asked where he was born and how he came to know Loretta, and he was happy to tell us. He came across as super-intelligent, and he was really full of himself. He wanted to show us he was smarter than us. Taw was very articulate. We just let him let it all out—the more they talk, the more they have to remember their lies."

As his police report notes:

Benderly reported that he attended Temple and Penn State universities, where he majored in Administration and Finance. He later worked as a CEO of IPEC, a petroleum corporation, owned by the lst National Bank. . . . Benderly stated he worked for IPEC for approximately nine years, spending the last two and a half years in Aberdeen, Scotland. He was brought in to clean up to books and revitalize the company. Towards the end of his time with IPEC, Benderly told us that he exercised $540,000 in stock options and all his money later went to zero, when the company failed. He did not pay United States taxes, but did pay British taxes.

Benderly stated he returned to Houston, Texas, where he hired an attorney from John Connelly's law firm, to help him recover some of his money. He only recovered $13,000 in equipment. By this time, Benderly said he was divorced from Deanna Burger and had two children with her. He told us that he lost contact with his children and his ex-wife died in 1998. Benderly reported he came to Phoenix in 1987 where his first position was as a patent engineer for Zerox [sic] corporation, as a vice-president. Benderly said he responded to an advertisement about a rental share in April of 1987. He met Loretta Bowersock and their friendship developed into an intimate one . . . Benderly said he worked for Bowersock's company by doing consulting work, reformulating merchandise and smoothing out their operation. Benderly reported that he was a major contributor to the success of the company.

Benderly said he also worked on lease negotiations, but by 1989, he decided to go into product development. He told us that he invented mowing equipment, sound equipment and had a total of 15 inventions, and holds patents for some. . . . Benderly said he is now involved with renewable energy and was supposed to have a meeting today with some people involved with a solar task force. When asked who the meeting was with, names, times, locations, Benderly told us that he had that information at his room, in his notes. He said he knows the director of energy services for the Tucson Unified School District, and as far as his meeting was concerned, it was to be an informal meeting lasting 1–2 hours. The time was open and he was to call in.

His tone and attitude made it obvious to the officers that this man thought he had more important things to do than sit at the Tucson police station answering questions.

Pacheco would later discover Taw didn't just lie about the big stuff—the entire education and work history he'd given them was fabricated—but about little stuff, too. While he finally admitted that he'd been married before—a significant piece of information he'd never shared with Loretta or her family—he'd lied when he reported his ex-wife had died.

But the crucial words were what he had to say about the last time he saw Loretta. As Pacheco later wrote in his report on the case:

Benderly reported that he dropped Loretta off at the south entrance of Dillard's and was driving in their red Dodge Caravan. When asked why the vehicle did not appear in the video surveillance, he said he had no idea. . . . Benderly said he returned to Park Place Mall at approximately 1555 hours [3:55 p.m.] and waited in his car until 1620 or 1625 hrs. When he did not see Loretta come out of Dillard's, Benderly went into the store . . . Benderly stated he entered through the south doors and began looking for Loretta in the men's section, in case she was buying him a gift. Benderly reported that he traversed both floors of Dillards, and after searching for 30 minutes, he went to the customer service desk, where he told them he could not find his wife and asked them to page her. After paging twice, Benderly told us that Dillards security, as well as Park Place Mall security, became involved in the search. Eventually, he called Tucson police from Dillards.

So how were things with you and Loretta? the detectives casually asked.

Benderly described his relationship with Loretta as good, but did have its ups and downs. Their conflicts were of a gentle nature and he added that he has never touched her in anger. He normally clams up during arguments.

There were so many inconsistencies and outright fabrications in that story that the detectives would have lost track if they hadn't been taking notes. But they clearly had a fish on the line, and after listening to all this for nearly two hours, it was time to get down to business.

Good police work—both in Tucson and Tempe—had already gotten credit-card information from the outlet mall and Love's, and police already knew Taw had it backwards—from Phoenix, you arrive at the outlet mall *before* you get to Love's, and to do it the other way means you have to backtrack on a freeway.

Police already knew Taw had actually been buying gas at Love's forty minutes *after* he claimed he was almost seventy miles away at a Tucson hotel.

Police already had the computer records of the check-in time at the hotel, and it wasn't 12:30 p.m., it was 2:48.

Police already knew the "traveling clothes" he'd described for Loretta were not among the few items of her clothing found inside the hotel.

Police already had seen the video from Dillard's and no matter how much they looked—they ran through the tapes a couple times to be sure—nobody matching her description ever walked into the store.

Taw hadn't searched high and low for her, they showed. Instead, he'd walked in the south door of the department store and gone directly to the customer service desk to report her missing.

Police already knew Benderly had both his and Loretta's passports, and although he'd told Terri he was going to Mexico for a week, he now changed his story and told Pacheco he'd been on his way to New Mexico to search for geodes.

"As smart as he thought he was, he was dumb in all these respects," Detective Pacheco notes. He and his partner sat there like satisfied cats listening to the pile of lies Taw Benderly was telling, and then Pacheco looked him right in the eye and told him his story didn't hold up.

"I gave him all the outs," Detective Pacheco recalls. "I said, 'Hey, something happened, it was an accident, was it self-defense? We all make mistakes, did you lose your temper?'" He remembers Benderly sitting there shaking his head in denial.

"I think Loretta's dead, and I think you know what happened," Pacheco said in a firm, but calm voice—the kind of voice police use as they nail you to the wall. "If you care as much as you say, you'll help us find her and not have her out there in the cold." Pacheco remembers: "It got really confrontational towards the end, but he was still in denial. He was totally convinced he was capable of getting away with it. He thought he was smart and articulate, and he thought he could explain it all away. But once he reported her missing, he was boxed in."

"I'm a gentle man—I don't kill bugs," Benderly

declared at one point. "I pick them up and take them outside."

Detective Pacheco then walked Benderly through every single item uncovered so far that pointed at his guilt:

—His timeline of leaving Tempe and arriving at Love's didn't match up to the actual times recorded on credit-card records: "I'm wondering if my watch was off. I just set it two hours ago," Benderly responded.

—The check-in time at the Tucson hotel was wrong. "Oh, for God's sake, I am totally confused," Benderly protested, and then told officers he wasn't "prepared to account for time point by point."

—There was a "large disparity" between the amount of clothes packed for Taw and those for Loretta. Benderly answered that Loretta had complained on the way down that she'd forgotten to pack some of her clothes.

—He was carrying a suspiciously large amount of cash. Benderly said he and Loretta had been planning to "surprise Terri" and pay her back the $20,000 they owed her, although he found nothing strange in carrying around all that money for a week-long trip where they wouldn't be seeing Terri.

—Why did he have two new cell phones? Benderly claimed they were for Loretta's grandnephews in Dallas and admitted they had just been purchased on Tuesday.

—Why did he have a dirty shovel and pick in the back of the red van? Benderly claimed they were going to be used later in the trip when he and Loretta dug for geodes.

—Why was he carrying his passport? Benderly now denied he ever intended to go to Mexico, and said he'd been headed for New Mexico, but always liked to carry his passport.

—Where'd you get the scratch on the top of your right hand? Benderly said that had happened last weekend when he was moving exercise equipment in his home.

Pacheco later wrote in his summary report:

I asked Benderly if he would be willing to submit to a polygraph exam. Benderly agreed to take a polygraph but since he stated he had not slept in two days, we agreed to postpone the polygraph for the next day. I asked Benderly if he would voluntarily turn over his three firearms and passport to us. Benderly told us that he would give us his passport but did not want to turn over his firearms. Benderly then demanded his car back and I told him that we were still processing the vehicle.

At 8:45 p.m., almost four hours after they'd started questioning him, detectives took Benderly to the Identification Section in the Tucson Police Department to be fingerprinted, photographed and sampled for DNA. They let him leave in his van, but followed him back to the hotel, where Benderly handed over his and Loretta's passports.

But the next day, Pacheco had yet another item to add to Benderly's list of lies: He'd called the Southwest Institute of Healing Arts, where Loretta often went for massages to help her osteoporosis. Director John Schultz checked with all three branches of

his school—Tempe, Phoenix, Scottsdale—and reported "he could not find any record of her receiving a massage on the morning of December 14."
The last time the Tempe school had seen her was
October 6.

First thing Thursday morning, Detective Pacheco
got a search warrant approved by Pima County Superior Court Judge Richard S. Fields, and at 9:57 a.m.,
he was at Taw's hotel room to seize his laptop computer, firearms and ammunition, financial documents
and "personal effects belonging to Loretta Bowersock."

On Friday, he met with Loretta's sister, Shirley
Gates, her husband, Sid, and her nephew, Matt Neal,
a policeman from Kansas. "Mrs. Gates told us that
her family has always distrusted Taw Benderly and
they even asked Loretta to leave him but she would
not," Pacheco noted in his report. Later that day, four
Tempe officers drove down to Tucson to meet with
Detective Pacheco about the investigation.

By now, the pile of lies was even taller. Benderly
told Pacheco about their white van breaking down
on Saturday, and claimed Loretta had driven him to
pick it up at the Cobblestone Auto Spa around 5 p.m.
on Monday. But police found mechanic Alex Janicsek, who set them straight about Benderly showing
up alone and claiming Loretta was home sick.

A closer search through Loretta's things at the
Tucson hotel showed that her reading glasses were
inside the messy makeup bag, wrapped in a tissue
paper. Terri told police her mother couldn't read a
thing without those glasses.

"I think Loretta was catching on to him and she

must have told him, 'That's it.' He snaps and kills her, and then he has to come up with a plan," Detective Pacheco surmises.

It might have started out as a clever plan—give yourself a five-day head start with an alibi—but it had fallen apart somewhere along the way, and why will forever be a lingering question in this case.

Detective Pacheco thinks arrogance eventually destroyed Taw Benderly: "He was a con man. He was a manipulator. He never accepted any responsibility or admitted what he'd done. But he thought he could get away with it."

He knew it was fruitless, but Detective Pacheco contacted the National Center for Missing Adults anyway. They put out a poster labeling Loretta an "endangered missing adult."

But Detective Pacheco already knew it was far worse than that. Because police had already scoured Loretta's Tempe home, and what they'd found there was like a punch in the gut.

CHAPTER 5

Secrets at Home

It's called a "welfare check," and it's designed to get a policeman at your front door to be sure you're OK.

That's the first thing Tucson police wanted once they were presented with the "missing person" named Loretta Bowersock. When it became obvious she wasn't somewhere inside the Dillard's store in Tucson—when hours had passed and she hadn't shown up and nobody had tried to contact anyone about ransoming her—police immediately thought of having her home in Tempe checked.

Perhaps Loretta had made her way home after skipping out on Taw, or perhaps there was something inside the house to explain where she'd gone. Taw had given police permission to enter the house, and they took him up on the opportunity.

Tucson found that two of its homicide detectives were in Phoenix on another case, and asked if they'd go over with Tempe police to check things out. The officers had no idea as they approached the house if they were going to be greeted by its owner, or if they were entering a crime scene.

Tempe detective John McGowan later noted in his police report:

The residence was entered, with the assistance of a locksmith. No signs of a struggle were initially noted, but upon checking inside a White Van parked in the garage, a long Grey hair was observed on the rear storage area of the Van. The rear seat had been removed and there was a large piece of cardboard lying on the floorboard. A black purse was then located rolled in a towel next to a box of towels in the back of the van. It was discovered that this was Loretta's purse.

As they opened the purse, officers immediately turned to each other and knew they needed a formal search warrant. This was more than a "welfare check," they recognized, and they needed a court-sanctioned search warrant to assure that anything they found as evidence of foul play would be admissible in a court of law.

"That we are doing this does not imply any wrong-doing in this case," Tucson sergeant Carlos Valdez told the *Tucson Citizen*. "We just want to be sure that if we do find evidence, that it was obtained lawfully."

The "affidavit for search warrant" said police wanted to collect any blood, hair or DNA evidence inside the house, as well as

two pairs of shoes and nylon rope, located in the garage on the east side of the residence; purse, with mis-cellaneous contents, which belong to Loretta Bowersock; computers, life insurance and financial information; mail; phone records and computers.

Officers told the judge about what had happened in Tucson the day before and what had already been

learned from Taw. Police had also found one neighbor home that morning and learned Loretta hadn't
been seen by them for some time.

*The Mom thought that strange, since Loretta normally
always takes care of plants in the yard. Taw had also recently borrowed $8,000 from the husband of this neigh-
bor. He didn't want the check cashed prior to this Friday,
12-17. Taw had told this neighbor that Loretta is still sick
and has the flu.*

The judge issued the warrant, effective at 10 p.m.
that night.

By the time officers gathered to execute the search
warrant, this had become a hot story in Arizona. Tucson
detective John Thompson noted in his police report:

*The cul-de-sac that this residence was located on had
been blocked to pedestrian and vehicular traffic by patrol
cars and yellow crime scene tape. Several news stations
were present, and appeared to be filming news segments.*

Officers entered the house, wearing gloves and
booties so as not to track anything in or leave behind
their own fingerprints. "Upon my entry into the residence, I noted that the house was fully furnished and
appeared to be very clean and tidy," Thompson later
wrote. Officers found a "suspicious stain" on the
garage floor—a blotch of red the size of a quarter—
but upon closer inspection, they discovered it wasn't
blood, but stain from a red flower.

Thompson's report continued:

The residence in question is a one-story house located on the south side of a cul-de-sac. Upon entering the front door, I found myself within a tiled breezeway which led off into three different directions. To the east was a dining room that continued on into the kitchen. To the south was a family room with an entry to the master bedroom and other bedrooms. To the west was a formal living room/sitting room.

The living room/sitting room appeared fully decorated with couches and chairs, as well as a writing desk in the northwest corner of the room.

Inside the desk, they found Taw's checkbook for his Bank of America account, as well as business cards, including one that listed him as president of T.A.W. Development Co.

Detective Thompson moved on to the master bedroom.

This room contained what appeared to be a queen sized bed with two nightstands, a dresser, a large mirrored wardrobe unit, chairs and a small table. A double door near the bed led out onto the back patio. The master bathroom contained a double sink with draws, as well as a separate toilet/shower room. The master closet was a walk-in, with clothing and shoes contained within.

Here they found a white hairbrush with long white hairs that they suspected were Loretta's.

This brush was maintained in the event the hairs would be needed for subsequent DNA testing or comparison. It should be noted that within the large mirrored wardrobe unit, there were numerous blankets and towels stacked on all of the available shelves. However, there was a space on one shelf that appeared uncharacteristically empty, as if a blanket or two had been there in the past.

Police would later find those blankets, matching some of the others still in the closet, in the back of the red van that at this moment was parked outside a hotel in Tucson.

A search of the family room found "nothing noteworthy." The same with the formal dining room. The kitchen was clean, its refrigerator full of fresh food, the pantry well-stocked. In the hall closet, they found boxes of financial records. Evidence Item No. 15 was "a cardboard box containing numerous financial statements from Chase Bank of Arizona."

Next came the spare bedrooms—two used as offices for Loretta and Taw, and the other as the guest room. "Both [office] bedrooms had at least one computer in them as well as a desk, phone and file cabinets." Among the things they found inside Loretta's office was a magazine clipping entitled "Keeping the Peace" that began:

Legal experts say it's important for couples to be clear about finances, wills, possessions and health care decisions before they set up house-keeping together. . . .

The article became Evidence Item No. 24.

In Taw's office, they found a business prospectus and corporate paperwork; checkbooks and financial records, as well as "two books relating to the care and use of firearms: Shooter's Bible and Black Powder Handbook." The books became Evidence Item No. 30.

Item No. 32 raised eyebrows:

Miscellaneous business paperwork which was in a pile on the desk within this office. Upon reviewing the paperwork, there were documents in there that included a "Corporate Resolution of Technology Lab, Inc." in which it appears Loretta Bowersock (identified as secretary) was permitting Taw Benderly (identified as president) to make financial decisions regarding property investments (specifically including the property located on Abraham Lane, Phoenix). This document appeared to have been signed by Bowersock on 03-26-03 and was mentioned to expire on 12-31-04. It should be noted that this document was at the top of the pile of paperwork collected under this item number. Additional documents located in this pile . . . a letter from U.S. Bank Home Mortgage dated 10-17-03 stating that loan [number is blacked out] is "seriously delinquent" . . .

Taw also had in his office five leather handgun holders, a cleaning kit for a .44/.45 caliber weapon and a zippered vinyl case that appeared to belong to a large-framed handgun.

Meanwhile, other officers had collected the envelopes in the mailbox and samples of dirt from the front yard, back yard and side yard.

Officers worked throughout the night, until 5:32 a.m., collecting and documenting items they thought might be helpful in the case. Before the investigation was over, they'd fill out more than seventy-five pages of search warrant information covering nearly four hundred items.

But there were a few items that pretty much told them the whole story. Inside the white van that had just had its brakes fixed, they found a towel wrapped around a woman's black purse. Inside the purse were:

Loretta's driver's license.
Her credit cards for Macy's, Dillard's and Home Depot.
Her checkbook, with checks written on 12-10 and 12-11.
A pair of prescription sunglasses.

As detectives looked at their find, they didn't even have to say it out loud: just how does a woman go shopping without her checkbook or credit cards or identification? How does a woman go anywhere without those things, to say nothing of a five-day trip to Mexico? And who goes anywhere in sunny Arizona without their prescription sunglasses?

What was inside that black purse convinced them that they weren't dealing with a missing person. Loretta wasn't missing, she was dead. And there was no question who was responsible. He was sitting in Tucson, trying to explain all this away with his I'm-smarter-than-you swagger. Every police officer involved in this case knew the truth.

But what in hell had he done with Loretta's body?

CHAPTER 6

Burying Loretta

They found the map in the red van, an ordinary Arizona map, except this one had big circles around areas along Interstate 8 in Pinal County.

There's nothing out there. Just out-in-the-middle-of-nowhere spots, mountains, cactus and a few abandoned buildings. It is impossible to stand out there in the vast, empty desert, and believe one of the nation's largest cities is just a few miles to the north.

Police found a dirty pick and shovel in the van, too, and that was an "Oh boy" moment.

They had a missing woman who'd never shown up at the place she was supposed to have been, and a man with fresh scratches on his hand who'd lied about searching a department store for her.

Police had all that within the first couple of hours of Taw making the 911 call to report Loretta missing. One and one indisputably added up to two.

Within the first twenty-four hours, they had Taw's credit card records and could trace his trip from Phoenix to Tucson. What most interested them was that two-hour gap between the ball caps bought at the outlet mall and the Arby's sandwiches bought five miles away at the Love's Travel Stop. The map gave them a loud clue that the two hours had been spent somewhere along Interstate 8.

Within forty-eight hours, they had Taw's cell phone records, and now they were pretty sure what had happened. Taw had left the outlet mall and taken Exit 198 onto I-8, had driven down the road quite a spell and found an out-of-the-way place where he couldn't be seen from the highway.

There he had pulled Loretta's wrapped body out of the van—laying aside the things he'd been using to help conceal it—grabbed his pick and shovel, and made her an instant grave. It would have been hard work, because the ground around there is caliche, or *hardpan*—a hardened layer of calcium carbonate— and it's a bitch to dig through. Your best bet is to find a wash where water flows now and then, and the soil has been loosened a little by rocks rumbling in the stream. But even there, the most you could hope to be able to do would be to dig down a few inches— two feet would be pushing the limit of most adults.

The pick would do most of the work, loosening whatever allowed itself to be chipped free, and the shovel would just move away any disturbed ground. Temperatures were in the low 70s, not a very hot day by Arizona standards, but anyone would have sweated and grown weary from such an effort. Taw was hidden, so he could take his time.

Although he was the only live person there, we do know precisely how he spent some of that time.

At 12:05 p.m., he started talking to his dentist about getting his teeth cleaned. Actually, there were four calls between him and his dentist's office. The first was their call to him, which went to voice mail when he didn't pick up. Then he called them back. Apparently they were having trouble settling on an appointment time, because there were two more calls after that. They finally set the date for the following week.

At 12:31 p.m., he called Loretta's cell phone, apparently listening for any messages. Then he twice called his own cell phone seeking messages. The last call ended at 12:33 p.m.

Police found all seven calls indicated "the phone was stationary and used only within one cell site range." That means all the calls came from the same spot, all routed through a cell tower just south of the intersection of I-8 and Highway 84.

Was he standing next to her grave as he casually dialed his dentist's number? Or was he shoveling between calls? Did he call when he took a break from stacking rocks on her grave? Or was he sitting on the crude pile as he blithely talked about cleaning his teeth? No one will ever know, but police are thankful he was so conscientious about his dental hygiene. Because the only reason they could trace any of these calls was that Taw Benderly had phoned back. If he had simply let them go unanswered, police wouldn't have been able to retrieve his record.

But he did phone back and it gave police a general area where he had to have buried Loretta. Without that, they wouldn't have had any parameters. Even with that, they were way off in their searches. This isn't like being at the intersection of two streets—this is one massively large desert. One look is enough to tell anyone that if Taw Benderly didn't want Loretta to be found, luck and reality were on his side.

He had to be one happy man when that grave was filled in. There he was, out in nowhere, finally rid of a body that had been his fixation for the last few hours. Now it was covered up with soil and rocks, and could stay hidden forever. He had money in his pocket, plenty of valuables in the van and all his clothes. He could almost hear the twangy strains of a good mariachi band in Mexico.

He got back in the van, dirty and dusty now, and headed back toward civilization. Then he bought two roast beef sandwiches. He'd tell police that he and Loretta had eaten them in the car as they drove, but it's not clear he was looking for an alibi at that moment—he might have just been hungry after his morning of hard work.

He probably washed up in the Arby's restroom. A damp paper towel would have felt soothing against his hot and tired neck. He could probably already feel the ache in his muscles, and he'd complain about a sore back for days.

Then off he drove to Tucson and his missing-person story.

Within minutes of turning onto I-8, Taw Benderly drove past the Casa Grande Cemetery, where folks have received proper burials since the 1920s.

Most Mexican-American cemeteries are elaborately decorated and tended, because Mexican culture respects and honors death, and the Casa Grande Cemetery is a great example. There are bright flowers everywhere, mostly silk or plastic so they'll last all year. You can't find an unadorned headstone, for each is draped in crepe paper or beautiful cloth. Many graves have plaques hand-painted with loving tributes. The graves of children often have a tricycle or a doll or a stuffed animal.

Grandmothers and grandfathers usually have plaster statues of Our Lady of Guadalupe to look after them—the patron Saint of Mexico as well as the Catholic Diocese of Phoenix. Some graves have pictures of the deceased, and many have fencing and iron rails.

There's nothing scary or forboding or sad in a cemetery like this. Every November 2—All Soul's Day—the Day of the Dead celebration refreshes the graves for another year, with new bouquets to replace those faded out by a year's worth of Arizona sun.

This cemetery was filled that afternoon with families, bringing their brightly colored blankets to spread on the ground for picnics of beans, barbacoa and tamales. Special candies were made for this day, including sugar skulls the children love. As the families picnicked, they told stories about the deceased, sharing their favorite memories. Certainly, somebody brought a guitar and there was serenading for both the living and the dead. Marigolds are the live flowers brought for this occasion, because it's said they smell nice to the dead.

By December 14 when Taw twice drove past the Casa Grande Cemetery, the marigolds were wilted, but the silk and plastic flowers still looked brand new. They'd last most of the year.

No such adornment signaled the secret, lonely spot where Loretta lay, for in the Arizona desert in December, there aren't even wildflowers to pretend they're marking a grave.

CHAPTER 7

Splitting Mother and Daughter

Even before her mother's death, Terri had spent a lot of time musing about how their lives would have been different if Taw Benderly had never ridden up on that motorcycle.

She can detail her life in two periods: pre-Taw and post-Taw.

The pre-Taw years were the ones of growing up and starting the business. Not all that was rosy, of course. Terri had been an insecure child. While her learning disability had left deep scars, she also wrote in her journal that "I don't remember being held and loved as a child." She'd always thought her older brother, Scott, got more care and cooing from their mother. She remembers contentious teenage years with constant fights with her mom. "I closed off to you and ran away and ran away and ran away," she wrote in a letter to Loretta after the murder.

But by the time Terri was 18, everything had changed: her parents divorced, Scott went off to his own life, and it was just her and her mother. They seemed not only to have called a truce, but to have found the love they felt for one another. "We started tennis and we were friends and shared everything—this was our best time in life," Terri writes.

For the next eleven years, Terri and her mother had the kind of relationship most people would envy. They were like partners in life—Loretta always watching her daughter's back; Terri always looking out for her mom. That they'd become business partners, too, was like the icing on the cake. "Our trust was powerful," Terri writes. "I trusted you more than anybody. I loved you!!! And you loved me!!! Then we ran an ad and brought to us TAW."

She admits she's spent too many hours fantasizing about what today would be like if they hadn't run the ad, if Taw had never shown up. In her dream world, she and her mother would still be partners, and the consignment business would be reaping untold millions. "We always dreamed of making it big and shopping on Rodeo Drive and stuff like that, and we never had a chance to do that," Terri says. But in her dream world, both women have lavish homes and closets full of designer clothes, and Loretta has a jewel on every finger. Even more important, they'd have traveled the world together and seen beautiful sites around the globe. And there'd still be those Christmas mornings with second-hand gifts they'd giggle over—"I only paid a dollar for this, can you believe it?!"—and Loretta would still be her best friend and powerful ally, and her loving mother.

But then Terri awakens to the second part of her life—the post-Taw years. And the picture is oh so different.

It had been Terri's idea for her mom to rent out a room in the Tempe house: "Executive woman, big home . . ." Terri remembers it was both a practical and hopeful gesture: her mother could use the rent money, but was also hoping to attract a man to share her life. "My mother's generation believed in standing by your man. They weren't women who wanted to be alone," Terri says.

Loretta was very open and vocal about her unhappiness with being alone—she'd been divorced for a dozen years, and hadn't come close to a permanent relationship. She was torn by the futility of a seven-year affair with a married man—she knew it was foolish to spend her time with a man she could never have, but she always maintained he was the "love of her life."

That man was Rex Armistead, who came to Arizona as director of the U.S. Justice Department's Regional Organized Crime Unit after the high noon assassination attack on *Arizona Republic* reporter Don Bolles. Bolles, who remains an icon of American journalism, died days after the attack that blew apart his limbs. Although three men went to prison for the murder, they were all considered the "hired help" of the crime, and whoever ordered this hit has never been brought to justice.

Loretta and Rex met at a bar, and the attraction was instantaneous. "I did love her," he acknowledges, and praises what a good tennis player and "hard-working lady" she was. He got to know Terri, who was well aware how smitten her mother was over this handsome man, and they also became friends. After he was out of the picture and Taw had arrived, Terri once asked Rex to use his federal credentials to look into Taw's background. "I ran a check on him—he had an insignificant record in

Texas," Rex remembers. "If there was violence in his background, we could not detect it."

The last time Rex heard from Terri, she'd called to tell him her mother had been murdered.

That Terri went searching for Taw's background signals she had doubts about him. But that's not the way things started out.

"He was tall and handsome and charming and suave," she remembers. "Everyone thinks bad guys are nasty. Uh-uh. They're charming. He said he was an inventor who had no family, that he was raised by his grandmother, that he headed a company in Scotland and never was in trouble with the law." But more important, "He said he had a great invention that was going to make him rich, and he'd give Mom a piece of the action. Oh, and he also began to woo her and make her feel she was the most wonderful woman he had ever met. The first year was great. He was always impressing her with his ideas and inventions, and he even stepped in to help me a lot. He knew I had a difficult time with reading and writing, so he suggested I go to a special reading course at ASU, and he and Mom would run the business."

It was while at ASU that Terri and her teachers invented the visual spelling book that helped her learn to read. By the time she came back to the business four months later, she was far better equipped to run things, but found her company in "financial disarray."

As she recounts in a letter to her mother:

We gave up our power and thought this guy was smarter and better capable of doing things. But it was not

*with the same integrity that we had. We should have
checked on him THEN! We began fighting and he began
manipulating our thoughts.*

Terri and Loretta had been scrupulous about only
spending the money they made—it was a great point
of pride that their only loan had been from Loretta's
mother—but Taw felt no such constraint. "My employees were coming to me and saying, 'This isn't
right—he's doing something wrong,' and when I'd
tell Mom, she'd stand up for him and we'd have another fight." It seemed to Terri that Loretta always
took Taw's side—refusing to listen to anyone else and
certainly not listening to her daughter's concerns.

"Mother had always been my confidante," she
said later. "Being dyslexic, I'd call her and ask how
to spell this and what does that mean? I'm doing this
business without an education and she was always
there for me."

And then came a blow Terri had never foreseen. In
1987, her mother came to her and demanded a buy-
out. The offer was blunt—"You buy me out or we buy
you out"—and the message was clear: Taw and
Loretta were now partners, and Terri was the odd
woman out. She couldn't believe her mother would
so quickly abandon her—Taw had only been on the
scene for two years, and already, he was replacing a
long-standing mother-daughter partnership.

Thinking back on it, it's obvious Loretta knew
Terri would never walk away from the business—
creating her own company was her lifeline to deal
with the dyslexia, which was still there, although
better controlled. Terri couldn't walk away, fearing

lightning wouldn't strike twice—this was her one way to make a living. Of course, her mother knew that, but more important, Terri is convinced, Taw saw the big picture clearly, and smelled all the money a buy-out would mean for him.

And being ever helpful, Taw suggested they could save all those legal fees if he wrote up the papers himself, as a gift to the women. Terri either forgot or ignored her earlier disaster with this kind of "help"; Loretta insisted that Taw's legal papers would be just fine. So the women split ownership of the four stores they then had, with Terri agreeing to buy out her mother for $150,000—the equivalent of about $266,000 in today's money. She made monthly payments until she could satisfy the fee. She'd later tell her journal, "As fast as I would pay her monthly payments, Taw would go through it on one invention or another." And still he asked for more. He was hitting up Loretta's friends, and he never hesitated to ask Terri for more "investment" capital. Terri was leery of his inventing skill, even though he had all the diagrams and schematics that made it seem real; but she knew the wedge with her mother would be even wider if she didn't show faith in the man Loretta was so crazy about. "I invested money into his inventions," Terri notes. "I kept believing that it would help them get on their feet."

Officially, Loretta was supposed to be off selling real estate, but that never went anywhere, and except for buying and selling second-hand items, neither she nor Taw ever held another job. "Finances and our relationship had become very draining and distant," Terri told her journal.

She resented Taw's hold over Loretta and his use of whatever money their household could muster. But to salvage any relationship with her mother, she put on a brave face and tried to carry on. Taw, who clearly knew he was the winner here, always remained "a smiling, charismatic, intelligent man," she writes.

It took Terri five years to pay the buy-out fee. And then came a day in 1991 when Loretta so betrayed her daughter, it felt like "she died to me."

Here's how Terri details it:

She showed up at my house dressed up like Alexis of Dynasty, just dressed to kill and you could tell she had to be rehearsed to do this, and she said 'I'm still an owner.' She showed me those papers that Taw had done for us, which showed she was still part owner of the company. I said I don't care about those papers, YOU AND I KNOW I BOUGHT YOU OUT!!!!! So then she handed me a lawsuit for the company and walked out the front door. I fell to my knees and cried. I had just lost my best friend, my mother who helped me get through life and I lost the only job I knew how to do. My mother was no longer my mother.

In the letter she wrote after her mother's death, Terri calls this "the worst day of my life." She writes:

Looking in your eyes, it felt like that I was no longer your daughter and you had NO care or concern for me and that I was your enemy. It wasn't the money that hurt, it was the tie of our lives that was severed. I sat on the stairs and I cried in pain and I cut our ties and the one person who was my confident [sic] in life was gone! My mother as I knew her was over.

I was trying to make you proud of me and what I could do. I guess I should have shared more money with you but it seemed it always went to Taw anyway. The next year was lawyers and disconnect and pain. The fact you knew that we did a buy out but that Taw's words were stronger, our bond was gone, gone. We were no more a family. From that day our trust was over.

Loretta's own "personal history"—prepared as one of her self-realization exercises—notes that in 1987 "sold my half to Terri." Yet there she was five years later, claiming she still owned half the business and demanding another buy-out. She was able to do that because Taw had rigged the original buy-out papers, making them worthless. How he'd convinced Loretta to go along with this sham is a mystery, but it does underscore how much control he had over her.

"Taw had her convinced it was just business, not a personal thing," Terri says now. "It's mind-altering to live with someone. He was always home. He never left to go to work, he was inventing out of the house. We negotiated the settlement down to $100,000, and I started making payments again and we worked through it. But it was never the same." While she lays all the blame on Taw, it is hard to imagine any mother being that weak and manipulated against her own daughter.

Terri remembers not speaking to her mother for an entire year, as their attorneys battled things out.

But on Mother's Day in 1992, for the first time in her life, she sent her mother flowers. She didn't bother to include a card, but Loretta called, asking, "Do I have you to thank for these?" and used the opportunity to meet with her daughter.

The flowers turned out to be a turning point as the women started to mend the rift. Terri says it never healed completely, but things got better over the years. The second time Terri ever sent her mother flowers was the day Loretta was murdered. Terri would eventually find those flowers strewn about the garage at Loretta's home.

Eventually, Terri tells her journal, she had the nerve to ask Loretta and Taw why they hadn't just come to her for money, rather than the ruse of the second buy-out and threatened lawsuit. "Taw answered, 'Have you heard the story of the donkey trainer? The trainer with a sledgehammer hits the donkey between its eyes because you first have to get his attention.' I looked at him and said, 'The next time, just hit me between the eyes, it would hurt less.'"

The story tells a lot about Taw Benderly and how "entitled" he felt. He obviously saw Terri's money from the business as *his* money. What else explains the strange notion that he had to get her attention when he'd already gone through the first $150,000 in buy-out funds, as well as every cent of Terri's "investments" in his bogus inventions? This was a man without scruples, without boundaries, without decency. He was milking Loretta every month—more than anyone would ever know until after he was dead—and he was milking her daughter, too. And yet he wanted more. He apparently didn't care that his selfish actions would destroy this mother-daughter relationship, and in fact, seemed to gloat that it was he who had Loretta's ear, not Terri.

One night as Terri left her mother's home, Loretta followed her out to the car. "Why don't you just stop making those payments?" her mother said sheepishly, apparently finally ashamed enough of what she'd done to stop the money flow. Terri asked how Taw would take that, and Loretta said something like "I'll handle him." That was the last Terri ever heard about this extortion, and she gratefully stopped the payments after only a few thousand dollars.

As she talks about it now, Terri is still astonished that this episode even happened. But now she knows how portentous it was—this man had such hold over Loretta, he could make her do almost anything. "Over the years I continually saw her change and change and change—and it wasn't just the money. The betrayal hurt the worst. . . .

"But I knew she'd never leave him. She told me she didn't want to be alone and she was too old to start over."

Terri consoled herself that lots of families have bad apples they must contend with, and realized her mother wasn't the first woman to do foolish things for a man. She figured Loretta must be getting the love she so craved, and resigned herself that Taw would always be there.

Considering all they'd been through, things were actually going along pretty well in 2004. The business was thriving, the recognition kept rolling in, Terri had become Arizona's "Domestic Diva" and peace had been called in the family. Their first trip had been the Alaskan cruise, and it had gone really well. "You were so much fun and your smile made me so happy," Terri later wrote to her mother.

Terri had just started Christmas shopping, hoping this year she'd find something so perfect and so cheap, she'd win her mother's game.

And then it all came to a screeching halt on December 14.

Terri didn't want to believe her mother was dead—she hung on to a fine silk thread of hope far too long—but when reality hit, when she had to face the truth, she still found it inconceivable that Taw would have ever hurt her mother. Being a mooch was one thing; being a murderer was another . . .

So when the psychic called and laid out a motive for her mother's murder, Terri was dumbstruck.

CHAPTER 8

A Motive for Murder

"That's baloney," an angry Terri Bowersock spat into the phone. "There's no possible way."

It was two days after Loretta had gone missing, and Terri was owning up to the very real, very certain possibility that her mother was dead. She was at her corporate office in Phoenix, arranging for media interviews and getting pictures of her mother printed for flyers to go in all her consignment shops, and she was grasping at anything that might lead to some answers.

A friend had suggested she contact Mary Ann Morgan, an internationally recognized psychic who had worked on several high-profile cases, including the Natalee Holloway disappearance in Aruba that cable news had been obsessed with for months.

Some people would have laughed and discounted the idea, but not Terri. Maybe it was her dyslexia and how she'd overcome years of frustration and failure to master her reading skills; maybe it was starting from scratch and building a business empire; maybe it was just that she's an adventurous person, but she'd seen miracles happen in the past, and she prayed for one now.

So she called, leaving a message for the woman

whose radio show is a must for the true believers. Mary Ann calls herself a "spiritual medium and messenger," with the motto "Live in the Moment, and in this Moment I wish you Peace." She has a Web site full of accolades from people who say she's helped them connect with someone on the other side—many believe she has a special talent.

"Mary Ann brings new meaning to the words, 'Dream Team,'" wrote Dr. Gary Schwartz, the director of the Human Energy Systems Laboratory at the University of Arizona, which studies the paranormal. "She not only has exceptional psychic gifts and skills that have been documented under controlled laboratory conditions, Mary Ann has the capability to walk the talk and reveal to each of us how we can live full and spiritual lives. Her intentions are of the highest order."

"Mary Ann is a gift from God," wrote James Twyman, author and "peace troubadour." "Mary Ann is one of those rare people who can pierce the veil between this reality and worlds beyond," wrote astrologer and teacher Penny Thornton. "Mary Ann Morgan is a Talent with a capital 'T'. She continually amazes me with accurate predictions . . . She can give specifics that leave no doubt as to the Truth behind her gifts," wrote Scott Davis, Emmy Award–winning producer at 3TV.

Mary Ann called back right away.

But even with her impressive credentials, things didn't start off well.

As she listened to Morgan over the phone, Terri became more and more convinced this woman was a nut.

"She said she saw my mother's house in foreclosure," Terri remembers. "That's when I knew she didn't know what she was talking about. I told her, 'There's no way my mother's house would be in foreclosure. Mess with anything, but not with her house—it was her pride and joy.'"

Morgan listened patiently to Terri's anger, hearing her call the idea "baloney." And then she repeated the unbelievable news again. "I saw it all clearly," Mary Ann recalls. "There was a notice on the door. It said the bank was foreclosing on the house. It gave a phone number to call."

Terri refused to believe it, and continued to dismiss Morgan as a crank.

But police already knew the psychic was right. Although they hadn't disclosed the information—and wouldn't for several days—they knew the day after Loretta was reported missing that her house was in foreclosure.

As police conducted a "welfare check" to see if Loretta had made her way home to Tempe, they were surprised by a knock on the front door. "A realtor had arrived at the residence, during our search, and asked if the house could be viewed, since it was in foreclosure," a police report notes. "Mail was seen in the mailbox, which also reflected that the County had placed the house in foreclosure."

Tempe police also interviewed all the neighbors who were home on the Manhattan Drive cul-de-sac, and they got the same news from Michelle Pazsoldan, whose little girls thought of Loretta and Taw as "grandparent figures." As Detective Trent Luckow reported, Michelle would watch over their house when the couple went out of town on business, often to Denver:

Michelle said that just prior to Thanksgiving, she went over to Taw and Loretta's house to take door flyers off the front door and deliver their mail while they were again out of town. At that time, Michelle observed a manila envelope on the door with a "foreclosure notice." The notice provided telephone numbers and that the person could assist with the foreclosure process. When asked if Taw and Loretta spoke to her about the foreclosure of the house, Michelle said they never brought it up and she did not mention it to them because she considered it their personal business.

Police searches of the house found more evidence that this household had trouble paying the mortgage. An ominous notice from U.S. Bank in October 2003 declared, "Your Account is Seriously Delinquent." Loretta had written on the notice, "called on 10-20-03. Must send payments in separate envelopes."

The current letter from Wells Fargo bank was far more serious. "Trustee Sale Date Scheduled," it began and noted that the bank intended to sell her house on March 14, 2005.

"The Loan Recovery Program is a solution to stopping your current foreclosure and stopping your sale date," the notice offered, and implored her to take "immediate action."

If you'd told Terri her mother had two heads, she couldn't have been more astonished.

What the hell had happened here?

How could this possibly be?

She'd made so many loans to Loretta and Taw, certainly they'd been able to pay the mortgage. Loretta would never have squandered that money and let her house payment go. That would have been the first bill she honored every month.

And Terri's certainty about her mother's protection of the Manhattan Drive home proved accurate. When police found her checkbook, they saw that she'd faithfully written out the two mortgage checks every month: one for $909.91 as the first mortgage, and the other for $299.17 for a second they'd taken out to finance one of Taw's inventions. The checks were sometimes not written until the 15th of the month, as the "grace period" expired, but they were there every month, just as they should be. And every month, just as you'd expect, that money was deducted from Loretta's bank account.

But when police contacted the bank, they found those checks had never made it to the mortgage account.

It started becoming obvious what had happened—but how had Taw kept this information from Loretta for so long? "I knew he controlled the phones, but I had no idea he controlled everything," Terri says. "You couldn't have a conversation with Mother without him being right there—he always monitored the phone. But we found boxes of mail in that house, and I finally learned he controlled all the mail, too. She only saw what he wanted her to see." As one of Loretta's friends would later explain, handling the mail, both the out going and the incoming, was one of Taw's "helpful chores."

Every month, he'd take the envelope with the

house payment, as though he were going to post it, and instead "washed" the check and remade it out to himself. Then he cashed it. He did this month after month after month, for more than a year.

When the bank started sending warning letters to Loretta—"your account is seriously in arrears"—he hid those letters. Letter after letter after letter.

But where had that money gone? What had Taw done with it? This certainly had to be Loretta's first thought after she'd learned what was going on. Was this some of the money he'd produce now and then, telling her part of a deal had come through—keeping her always on the hook that maybe an invention was finally going to pay off? Was this money he spent on the "frivolous things" she complained that he liked to buy? Or perhaps he'd stashed it away somewhere as a hedge in case she ever actually got the nerve to throw him out—but that was simply a fantasy, because Taw never saved a dime of all that mortgage money.

What she'd thought of as his way of being helpful around the house had been his ruse so he could steal from her and keep her in the dark. What else had the unseen mail tried to tell her—what else had he stolen or squirreled away as his own private plan? Had there been anything else meant for her that he'd kept for himself? She would never know, but there was so much more.

Police already had learned where a big hunk of that money had gone: to the man who was Taw's business partner, Jerry Baughman—a man who thought he was in a legitimate business relationship with Taw Benderly and that they were lining up investors for solar energy projects.

Baughman was admittedly nervous when he was called in to the Tempe Police Department at 1 p.m. on Saturday, December 18. He'd never been questioned by police before, hadn't even been inside a police station until this moment. But he was more than willing to cooperate. He'd talked to his partner the day before and reported that Taw "sounded terrible."

The police report notes:

Baughman explained that Benderly spoke quietly and was difficult to understand. Benderly admitted that he did not have any sleep and he had been up watching the news. Benderly also said he was with family, which Baughman assumed was Bowersock's daughter, Terri, because Terri had been on the news from Tucson.

The two men had been partners for two years in a company called Integrated Energy Technologies, which intended to create an "energy system" that used solar energy with gas cooling to save 50 to 60 percent off utility bills.

When asked about money and funding for these projects, Baughman said Benderly had been "arranging money" for approximately 2 years. Benderly would arrange for investors to invest in the IET company, however Baughman never met any of them. Baughman was unaware about how much money had actually been invested. Baughman described a Non-Governmental Organization (NGO) which was formed from Canadian Investors. Benderly told Baughman that the NGO provides financing of the projects by giving Benderly money into his Bank of America account. Benderly was then to transfer money from his personal account into Baughman's account as payment for his work.

Baughman said Benderly "frequently traveled" to Canada to meet with these investors; sometimes going there from Kansas when he and Loretta visited her sister in Hutchinson. "Benderly had been traveling to Toronto, Canada almost every week for a month," Baughman told police, unaware that was not true.

When asked if he had been paid for the work he completed, Baughman acknowledged that he had in small amounts . . . He had collected approximately $50,000 to $60,000 over the past one and a half years. Approximately two weeks ago, Baughman was paid $10,000.

But Baughman also told police that money wasn't always there when it was supposed to be, and that he had financed some of the projects himself. Taw currently owed him $150,000 in back salary and expenses.

He told officers he had been waiting for a week for Benderly's promised payment of $40,000—when the money wasn't there, Benderly sweetened the promise by saying he would pay an additional $100,000 as a "bonus." But so far, Baughman hadn't seen any of this money.

The detective asked why Benderly was in Tucson in the first place, and Baughman repeated what he'd been told by his partner: Taw was going to meet with his Canadian investors, who planned to build a

50 megawatt solar power plant. Baughman would manage the plant, although he didn't know where it was being built or who any of the investors were.

Benderly once told him to let him worry about the finances and not get involved. Baughman would constantly tell Benderly to communicate with him more because he did not know what Benderly did on a day to day basis for the company.

Detective Luckow's report notes:

I asked Baughman if he believed Benderly was the type of person that had anything to hide, which he did not believe Benderly was. Baughman also did not think Benderly would lie to police either.... Baughman believed Benderly was an honest person and did not think Benderly knew where Bowersock was currently located. When asked if he knew where Bowersock was located, Baughman said "thank you, but I don't have a clue, I wish I did, if I did I would not be here."

Police were watching big pieces of the puzzle fall into place. Within the last two days of her life, Loretta had discovered that she was soon to be homeless. And just when she thought she was home free with the nest-egg house as the cushion she needed for her later years; just as she dreamed of sending Taw away—buying him off, actually, but most important, getting him and his money-sucking schemes out of her life; just as she was about to be able to pay back her daughter, who'd been so generous with loans along the way; just as a new life was there around the next corner—now she found that the very foundation of that life, the home she intended to be hers through her final years, was about to be auctioned off.

Loretta started calling Wells Fargo, praying there was some way she could derail this ruination. She undoubtedly was sitting at her desk in the den off the kitchen when she picked up the phone at 3:33 p.m. on Monday afternoon, December 13, and began seventeen consecutive calls to ten different bank phone numbers. But she was enraged and devastated when she finally hung up at 4:44 p.m. It had taken one hour and eleven minutes for her entire world to fall apart.

It's not known how she finally discovered the bank was about to foreclose. Taw had been able to keep this news from her for some time. Did a call come through that he didn't screen? Did a notice arrive on the door that he couldn't squirrel away? However it happened, Loretta shifted into full gear once she discovered what was going on. It's also not known what she learned in her pleading calls to the bank, but she was probably told she could save the house if she made all the back payments and the fees associated with the foreclosure action. It would have taken most of her new nest egg to do that. And then she'd be back in the same leaky boat she'd been frantically bailing out all these years.

Because Loretta still believed her financial windfall was safely in the bank.

The third thing that isn't known about her last hours is if she ever discovered that Taw had already squandered most of that $69,000 that had made the last week so joyous.

His "money-saving" scheme of wiring those funds into his business account—saving all those real estate fees—was his ruse to get his hands on every penny. At that moment, there was only about $24,000 left. It had taken him less than a week to spend most of it, although where he spent it is still a mystery.

Jerry Baughman later told police that on that Monday, as Loretta's world was falling apart, Taw was telling him the Canadian investors had wired $70,000 into Taw's Wells Fargo account. As soon as he could get the money shifted into his Bank of America account, Taw would be sending Jerry the $40,000 he was owed. The money should be in Jerry's account by Friday, December 17.

Police easily put two and two together: Loretta's $69,000 house profit was the same money Taw was passing off as a $70,000 investment from Canada. Had she discovered that, too, in her frantic phone calls, or was she spared that last indignity?

And now she had absolute proof that this man she'd pledged her life to, the man she'd done so much soul-searching and anguishing over, had been both lying to her and stealing from her like a common thief.

While Loretta was on the phone, Taw was at his desk, too, in the adjoining den, where he logged on to his Gateway laptop computer at 4:35 p.m., making a Google search for "loan star mortgage." It was the only time his computer was used that entire day.

Nine minutes later, Loretta's fury would have been at full volume.

Mary Ann Morgan told Terri she "saw" the murder even before she ever stepped inside Loretta's home. But after she went to the house with Terri right after Christmas, "it came through clearly."

"When Loretta found out about the foreclosure, he lost it," Mary Ann recounts. "He came up behind her and choked her. He pulled her into the hallway by the laundry room and she died there. That's where she crossed over. He's so angry, he took her out to the garage. In the garage I showed Terri the tarp—that's what she's wrapped in, I told her. And I showed her the tape gun—that's what he used to wrap up the tarp, I told her. I saw it so clearly, it was like watching a movie."

It would be a long, long time before Terri would discover that everything Mary Ann Morgan had just said was true.

CHAPTER 9

The End of Taw

It doesn't take a homicide detective to see that Taw Benderly had started with one plan, and in midstream, switched to another.

He clearly left the Tempe house never intending to come back, packed with clothes and valuables and a wad of cash, to say nothing of a cover story that gave him a week's head start to run.

How simple it would have been for him to drive straight through Tucson, continue down the road another sixty-four miles to Nogales, cross the Mexican border and disappear forever. It's a snap to vanish in America's Third World neighbor; easy to live a long, long time on just the cash in his pocket. How smart it would have been to sell the valuables he had in the back of the van—hell, sell the van itself for a nice piece of change, and meld into a casual life of an expatriate in a Margaritaville world.

Nobody would have even wondered where they were for a week, and by then, all tracks could have been erased. As far as anyone was concerned, he and Loretta would both have vanished without a trace, and to this day, no one would ever have known what happened to them. People would have suspected one of two things—either they ran away from their financial problems, or they were victims of foul play. Nobody would know for certain that Loretta was dead. Nobody would even guess she was buried in the desert. Nobody would know Taw was a murderer. Most likely people would guess the long-time couple from Tempe were still together, either both alive or dead.

After all, Taw was already practiced at disappearing. Unbeknownst to anyone who knew him now, he had already walked away from three families. Surely, he saw the opportunity and wisdom of doing it again.

But somewhere along the boring highway between Phoenix and Tucson, Taw Benderly changed his mind and decided to go with his missing-person ruse.

It's one of the big puzzlers of this story—Why did he do that? What could he possibly hope to gain? He already had most of their money and all their treasures; he knew the house was in foreclosure and expected the unpaid utility bills to result in turnoffs soon. He had to know Terri wouldn't rest until she found out what happened to her mother. He'd been in this family long enough to know Loretta's sisters would track every clue. He certainly knew Terri was a whiz at getting media attention—and the media loved this kind of story.

Of all the things Taw Benderly was, he certainly wasn't a stupid man. He had called police with a story in place and had fully expected them to buy it. Loretta was missing; he was as perplexed as everyone else. But if he was so smart, how could he have left so many conflicting clues? Did he actually believe he could explain away a two-hour gap in his schedule by saying his watch had stopped? Even as police started tearing his story apart, he kept making absurd excuses to explain all the discrepancies away. Or how about the complaint he voiced again and again? "That damn Scott Peterson case. Now they think that every man would kill his wife." He said it like it was downright insulting police would use guilt by association to suspect him, as though the *only* reason they were on his case was that a California jury had found 32-year-old Scott Peterson guilty of killing pregnant Laci and their unborn son.

Both of Loretta's children are convinced that his arrogance got to him. "I think he intended to run away, but on the drive to Tucson, he convinced himself he could get away with it," Terri says. "His lies had been so successful in the past, he got himself convinced he could pull it off." Her brother Scott agrees. In an email to his family he said,

He was a man that was always right—in his mind. He was very prideful of his knowledge and correctness on every subject. All religions have a saying about pride before the fall—his ego and greed were the downfall.

In a telephone interview from Hawaii, Scott adds: "He wanted to get away with it. I don't think he wanted to be on the run in Mexico. He was old. And he'd just murdered the woman he loved—yes, he did love my mother. He wasn't stupid, but he was a liar of great proportion. He was a know-it-all. He didn't come up with a good plan—he didn't have time. But

Taw liked reading mysteries and he wanted to go on with life and not be a hunted man."

Scott is convinced that Taw never dreamed Terri would jump in her car and speed down to Tucson. Terri herself says she thinks this surprised him, as though she'd have ignored such a thing. "My mother would have been just a missing person if it wasn't for my sister—she's the one who got the media involved," Scott notes, and even the media agree this is right.

Detective Pacheco thinks the Bowersock kids are on the right track: "He thought he was smart and articulate, and could explain it all away. He sure thought he was smarter than any police officer. But once he reported her missing, he was boxed in." Pima County Sheriff's detective Landon Rankin, whose office would search long and hard for Loretta, gives Benderly at least a human reason: "I think he didn't run because his conscience got ahold of him," he says. "But then he panicked, and in his panic, he made a lot of mistakes."

But an expert in criminal behavior, forensic psychiatrist Steven E. Pitt, says it's easy to see what happened.

"This man was a narcissistic sociopath—he was a self-engrossed, entitled person who thought he deserved preferential treatment, and the laws didn't apply to him. He thought he could get away with anything and could manipulate anyone—some of our best politicians have the same traits," he says. "There's a lot of people out there like Benderly—he's a con's con. He didn't keep going because he thought he could get away with it."

Dr. Pitt, whose sixteen-year-career has included work on Colorado's three big cases—the JonBenét Ramsey murder, the Columbine High School massacre and the Kobe Bryant rape case—says that Benderly's self-delusion isn't as unusual as it may seem. "First of all, a lot of people get away with murder—and don't forget, this guy conned people all his life. His narcissism tells him he's smarter than everyone else, and he's thinking he pulled this off. That bit about the watch being off two hours—that's a verbally skilled psychopath. He was good."

Loretta's sister Shirley Gates thinks there was no limit to his faith in his own cover story. "I think when she found out about the foreclosure, she tried to get him to leave, but he knew there was still money in the bank. And after he buried her, he knew there was still a deep pocket in Phoenix, and that was Terri." While that may seem preposterous—how could anyone think a daughter would support the man who killed her mother?—even her brother thinks that was part of the story. "My sister was still there to bail him out," Scott says, obviously unhappy that his sister had become an enabler by her frequent loans. "My sister holds blame here, too." Besides, Taw had proven in the past he thought he could con anyone out of anything.

His actions in the days after reporting Loretta missing show that he'd bought his own BS—he truly thought he could dodge this crime. After all, there was no body, and without a body, maybe Loretta really had been kidnapped at Dillard's.

Taw Benderly started out the morning after Loretta's disappearance—Wednesday, December

15—with another shock for Terri. "We went to his room to get him and he said, 'Oh, by the way, your mother wanted me to give you this money—it's $20,000 to pay you back for the down payment on the house.' " Terri remembers looking at the wad of cash as though it were poison, and asking him, "You mean you brought all this cash on vacation with you to give to me when you got back from your vacation?" She remembers he acted as though there was nothing unusual about that, as though that was a perfectly logical reason for carrying such a wad.

Taw also insisted on calling Scott again in Hawaii, telling him, "I guess they got her," before handing the phone over to Terri. What's going on? Scott asked, and Terri reported Taw's insistence that they had been followed by a "suspicious van" the day before. She told her brother she'd call later when she had any news. Scott Bowersock would never hear Taw Benderly's voice again.

Terri remembers she wanted desperately to go back to Dillard's, to search some more, and Taw said he wanted to go, too. As they got to the red van in the parking lot of the hotel, Taw told Terri to take some of the valuable paintings inside for safe keeping. "I reached in and pulled back a coat and saw a pick and a shovel," she remembers. "He covered it up and said, 'Oh, that is just in case we have car trouble.' " Terri would learn later that he'd excused the pick and shovel to police as "geode-digging" equipment, but he didn't even bother using that lie on her, because she knew they would never go digging for geodes.

She thinks now that their "search" of Dillard's that day was a way for Benderly to check that the store's security cameras didn't extend to the parking lot. He had to realize by now that the in-store cameras wouldn't show Loretta arriving at all—and later in the day, police would confront him with that evidence. So now he advanced a new alibi to explain all that away: "I dropped her off and drove off, she must have been kidnapped in the parking lot."

Terri kept fighting the growing fear that he had done something awful to her mother—she clung to the hope that the woman had indeed been kidnapped and would be found and saved. She couldn't bring herself to imagine the alternative. But when she went down to the Tucson Police Department that afternoon, all the signals from the officers were that she was fooling herself. At one point, she called her brother. "Ask the questions," she told him over the phone, and Scott picked up right away that she couldn't talk because Taw was around. "Is he sitting right next to you?" he asked his sister. "Uh huh," she answered. "Is he the number one suspect?" Scott asked. "Uh huh," Terri said. "And then I knew my mother was dead," Scott says.

But others who knew Taw were having a helluva time imagining him as a killer.

"I considered him my friend, too," Lorraine Combs would later say. "I never suspected this could happen. There wasn't a clue." The woman who'd spent Saturday night with Loretta and Taw over dinner and a Christmas light tour, heard about Loretta's disappearance from her son Bill. He'd heard it on the news Wednesday afternoon and couldn't believe it—he rushed to the Manhattan Drive house, to find television and newspaper crews already there.

"Taw was always friendly with my whole family, and I had nothing against him," Combs says. Loretta had never shared any concerns about Taw, and from what Combs knew, they were a happy couple. "I knew there was a rift with Terri, but that was all."

Lorraine's daughter, Diane Hanson, even called Taw at one point, asking if there was anything she could do to help him. She told police he was hard to understand, but warned her not to let the media reporters "push you around," and told her he might need a place to stay. "He told me when a woman comes up missing, you automatically know who the suspect is," she told police, and he added, "Well, I hope she pops up." She remarked to police that Taw "spoke in a very casual mode, which was unusual for him."

It was Hanson who told police that when they'd had dinner Saturday night, Taw didn't have a scratch on his right hand, as he did when he'd shown up in Tucson. She remembers specifically because after dinner, he'd shown her some quilts and "she was able to see his hands during that time."

Businessman Gary Bailey, who talked to Taw almost every day, never once considered that he might have hurt Loretta. "There was no way he killed Loretta, I thought when I first heard," he remembers. "His partner, Jerry [Baughman] called and said, 'They can't find Loretta,' and I said, 'How do you lose Loretta?' She and Taw were absolutely two of the nicest people I had ever known in my life. I knew Taw was meeting with people out of Canada about a project in the desert, and I thought maybe those people had kidnapped her." Bailey tried calling Taw's cell phone to find out what was going on. He always got the brushoff and Taw's promise of a return call that never came.

Skyla Petersen had no such delusion—in fact, she had a good idea how bad it was inside that house, and had severed her twenty-year friendship with Loretta because she couldn't deal with how Taw "sucked Loretta into a psychological trap." But even Petersen would not have guessed he was violent.

Skyla later learned another friend had once advised Loretta to be careful because of Taw's temper. "But I never saw that side of him," she says. "He didn't have a temper, he didn't use swear words, neither he nor Loretta were drinkers." And so she didn't think Taw had hurt Loretta. She clung to the hope that Loretta had just taken off, and would someday show up, safe and sound. "You never want to think the worst," Skyla says. But the more she learned, the more she knew she was avoiding the reality. "She would probably have thrown him out rather than leave her home," Petersen says. "So maybe she broke and was throwing him out. And he had no place to go."

Ursula Kramer, whose long-time friendship included regular weekly telephone chats with Loretta, never saw violence coming, either. And, she told police, neither had Loretta.

"I don't think Taw had ever hit her," Kramer said in a police telephone interview. " 'Cause I asked her one time . . . and she said no. She says he may have come close to it, but no. She never believed that he would hurt her, as far as I know. And I never really saw Taw to be super-violent, either." In fact, the one who was on the "abusive side," Kramer said, was Loretta. "A little verbally abusive, and actually, you know what? Between you and me, I used to sometimes think to myself, Loretta, why are you talking to him like that? Yes, maybe, you know, things aren't so good and this and that . . .

"But she would get really nasty. . . . sometimes an assault on his male ego. And she would do it in front of me."

Meanwhile, Loretta's sisters waited with dread. "The first thing we all felt was he'd killed her," Darla Neal remembers. "There was no chance Loretta had run away. Loretta didn't run. Taw called me and went through his song-and-dance crap. He started to cry when he said he was a suspect. My son, Matthew, noted he only cried when he talked about his own problems—he didn't cry about Loretta. Matthew said that's what he'd expected, that Taw only cared about himself."

The sisters weren't the only ones who instantly laid blame. So did the attorney who'd handled legal issues for Loretta and Taw for years. Michael St. George remembers "the feeling was so strong" that Taw was a murderer. "My secretary walked in and said, 'He killed her,' and I said, 'Yeah, he did.'"

St. George had known Loretta before Taw was ever in her life, remembering her as "an absolutely classy lady, very likable, very sociable." And he could easily see her attraction to Taw. "Taw was incredibly charming, gifted, intelligent, a wonderful conversationalist and he was a good-looking fellow. I met him when he was about fifty and he was physically fit to the max.

He was kind of exciting to be around. He could talk snow off a snowball. He was a quick study, and relentless. He worked day and night."

St. George says he was always astonished that someone so smart never made it: "Is it a shame he didn't use his talents to become a success? Shame doesn't even begin to describe it. It was awful. He was an extremely capable guy, and I couldn't put my finger on why he couldn't make things work."

But St. George also knew the other side of Taw, witnessing several times the "vicious temper" that was downright scary. And the other thing he knew about Taw—the overriding memory he has of the man—is also the reason Taw didn't run: "He firmly believed he was smarter than anyone on the face of the earth."

Taw's friend Gary Bailey agrees: "What was so bizarre is that here was all that talent and all that potential, and it never worked. Was he so unorganized he just went from one thing to another? I'll never know."

Benderly stayed at the Tucson hotel until Thursday morning, December 16, then drove back to Phoenix and checked into the Residence Inn at the airport at 1:25 p.m. He got room 357 and signed in under the name "Bob Smith." He told Terri he didn't want to go to the house because there was too much media presence. The story was hot with coverage on all the television stations and Valley newspapers. Terri was constantly being interviewed, and TV crews went with her as she drove out to the desert— searching in places that psychics had "seen" her mother's body.

On Friday, Benderly went looking for legal help.

The first thing that impressed family law attorney Robert Baumann is how "nattily dressed" Taw Benderly was: blazer, turtleneck sweater—reminiscent of the TV character Ted Baxter of *The Mary Tyler Moore Show*. "He was perfectly coifed, and the way he walked, with a false sense of suave—that's what Taw was like," Baumann says.

"He had a surprisingly impressive bearing about him and he had a beautiful voice," Baumann remembers of the man who walked into his office at 44th Street and Thomas Road. "What brings you in today?" Baumann asked, and Benderly went right to the point: "My wife is missing . . . I dropped her off at the mall . . . I called Terri and she came down . . . I gave Terri twenty thousand dollars' cash . . . now I've got police following me . . . they're asking about the shovel in my truck . . ." The story kept getting stranger by the sentence.

Baumann already knew the answer to the next question, but he asked anyway. "Are you a suspect?" Benderly admitted that he was, because "police followed me all the way from Tucson to Phoenix."

"The story just seemed incongruous," Baumann says. "What was all this money he gave Terri, what was this shovel? He acted like it was a routine thing because he and Loretta went digging, but this wasn't the kind of guy who'd get his hands dirty. He said he and Loretta had seen funny characters in Tucson and thought they were being followed. His timing was all off, but he blamed it on his watch being off. But he'd just told me he bought and sold fine watches that are expensive and accurate. He had an explanation for everything. It disturbed me, but I looked at him with a straight face. It was kind of surreal."

Taw then started questioning Baumann to see if the lawyer was up to his standards. "He went into a soap box kind of discussion on how he needed someone to represent him who was a firm believer in the right of privacy, who believed in due process." Then he launched into a bragging fest about his inventions, although Baumann was never clear on exactly what he'd invented. "He left me with two impressions: that he was very impressed with his own knowledge and that his inventions were important. And he sure didn't leave me with the impression he was dirt poor."

Baumann said he'd be happy to call the police and find out the status of the case. "He throws a credit card on my desk with a flourish, as though money were no object. I told him my regular retainer is two-fifty an hour and he said, 'Say we put a thousand on the card.' It was unusual, but it fit his blustery personality."

The meeting lasted about an hour. The next day, Baumann called police, who filled him in on more details, and the attorney clearly saw that "the story didn't fit together." Baumann called Benderly a couple of days later, trying to get more details. "We have a confidential relationship," he told him. "You can tell me anything." Police hoped Baumann could shake the truth free and get Benderly to give himself up, and the attorney agreed to try.

He called Benderly a second time and tried to get him to come into the office again, but no luck.

In the meantime, Taw started putting his affairs in order. On Saturday, December 18, he called and left

a message for one of Terri's business associates, asking him to come to the hotel Sunday morning and
pick up items he was leaving for Terri at the front
desk. Kevin Crippa would later tell police that Taw
also told him, "Loretta and I said we would be with
each other for eternity. I miss her." It was the first
time anyone had heard any sense of loss from him
over Loretta's disappearance.

Crippa told Terri about the call and she insisted
that she should go along. She asked Crippa to come
by her house early Sunday morning and they'd go
over together. He reminded her that psychics had
been telling her Taw was dangerous and "she was to
stay away from him." She reminded her friend she
wouldn't be alone.

But on Sunday morning, when Terri and Crippa
called Taw's hotel room—three separate times—
there was never an answer, and they worried something was very wrong. Terri called police as she and
Kevin rushed to the hotel.

At the front desk, she found Taw had left her several things:

—Two copper paintings, valued at about $40,000.

—A briefcase with the keys to the red van parked
outside and an ominous computer-written note in
cursive style:

*Loretta and I vowed over the years that we would
spend eternity together, and so we shall.*

—A notarized document titled "immediate transfer of ownership and control" that read:

*On this 18th of December, 2004, I, Taw Benderly, be-
ing of sound body and mind, do hereby transfer to Terri
Bowersock, ownership of and access to, and immediate
control of all my worldly tangible and intangible assets,
and it is my intention that this Immediate Transfer of
Ownership and Control shall immediately supersede any
Wills or any other previously executed legal documents.*

He listed seven items, including his Wells Fargo
bank account, which still contained about $11,000;
his PayPal MasterCard with $2,500 in credit, jew-
elry; wristwatches; his Sony notebook computer;
and all his clothes. He also left her his interest in
three inventions:

*My audio-transducers—"Concert Walls"; my
lawn mowing technology—"Swift Cut," and my heat
resistant shading fabric for automobiles—"Covered-
Parking."*

It scared both Terri and Kevin that Taw was about
to leave this world. She called his room from the
lobby. "I could hardly understand what he was saying, and he was slurring his words," she remembers.
"He sounded very drugged." Now she was sure he
was trying to commit suicide—had probably already
taken an overdose of pills—and at her urging, Kevin
called the police.

Units from both Phoenix and Tempe rushed
to the four-story hotel on 44th Street. By the time
Tempe's homicide detective Trent Luckow arrived, Terri was sitting outside near a cement table.

He remembers her being "frantic" with worry that Benderly would kill himself and they'd never discover where Loretta was buried. She begged to get into Taw's room so she could talk to him, but Luckow refused to allow it.

Then she told Luckow about the items left at the desk. She had put them in Kevin's trunk and he'd already left—he was heading south to help organize another search party in the desert. The unhappy detective asked her to bring the items back, because they were evidence in the case.

Leaving Terri to cool her heels, Luckow went up to Taw's third-floor room. In the hallway, he found several officers who filled him in on what was happening.

His police report notes:

Upon police arrival it was learned from hotel staff that Benderly had been wandering the hotel hallways attempting to get into different rooms and appeared lethargic. A Phoenix Police Tactical team responded to the hotel in order to get Benderly from the room, which they were able to do. Benderly was then moved to room #358 in order to be treated by Phoenix Fire Paramedics. Officer Gregory Gibbs explained that Benderly used his credit card when he checked into the hotel, however the hotel staff checked him in using the name "Bob Smith" based on the media attention of this case.

I then interviewed Phoenix Police Officer Ron Dorfman who negotiated via telephone with Benderly. Benderly told Officer Dorfman that he did not want to hurt himself and did not want to hurt anyone else. Benderly agreed to exit his hotel room and be contacted by police and paramedics.

Taw told them he had just taken extra cold medicine and that's why he seemed so groggy. Their examination found nothing to the contrary.

Detective Luckow also questioned Kristen Owszarzak, who was working the front desk at the Residence Inn. She told him Benderly "looked sick and he stumbled while he walked 'like he was going to throw up.'" Benderly had told her he had the flu. She remembered his skin was yellow and he had bags under his eyes.

Although Tucson police had already searched the red van, Luckow wanted another search, and officers went off seeking a warrant. Besides the van, they asked the judge to let them search Taw's hotel room. They got both warrants later that day and, getting the keys to the van from Terri, police impounded it and towed it to the Department of Public Safety lab in downtown Phoenix.

Among the pieces of evidence they collected from the van were "sticks and stems from unknown vegetation" in the undercarriage of the van, indicating that it had recently been driven in the desert. At the lab, officers would also find a recent dent in the undercarriage and many soil and seed samples in the passenger cabin.

Meanwhile, Luckow and other officers searched Taw's room. Evidence Item No. 65 was the black baseball hat Taw had bought at the outlet mall on the way to Tucson. Evidence Item No. 70 was a collection of "miscellaneous CD data disks" found in a black bag on the bed. Evidence Item No. 72 was the paperback book *The Last Juror*, which Taw had bought at Costco on his way back from Tucson (they found the receipt for the book, too). Evidence Item No. 73 was a get-well card from the Residence Inn. Evidence Item No. 74 was a number of "newspaper articles on missing person Loretta Bowersock."

By the time they were done searching the room, Terri had returned with the items from Kevin's trunk. Although it isn't included in any police report, Terri says she "made a deal with police—I gave them the things Taw had left for me and they let me go in to see him. I knew, I just knew, I could get him to tell me where she was."

If police had known what she'd intended, they'd never have permitted the visit. "The police didn't know it, but I went in to make him a deal," she recalls. "He was the only contact I had with my mother, and I was ready to do anything to find out where she was." She remembers walking to the door of his room with dread, but also with hope. She wasn't exactly afraid of him—despite the warnings from the psychics—but she had to screw up her courage to enter that room. She remembers that when she came through the door, he'd reached back and locked it. He gave her a hug. She waited until he turned away and then surreptitiously unlocked the door. They sat on the sofa in the suite. "His hair was all messy and I combed it back with my fingers," she remembers. "I said, 'Tell me where she is and I'll get you out of this.'" She admits she was ready to keep her word, even knowing she'd be bucking the law, and would have smuggled Taw Benderly out of Phoenix if he'd have 'fessed up.

"I told him I could get him a car and money and out of town before anyone knew, just tell me where she is. I was ready to promise him anything."

Loretta and Dave Bowersock in 1954—a marriage that wouldn't last.   Courtesy of Terri Bowersock

Loretta holding Terri in 1956.

Courtesy of Terri Bowersock

Loretta with her sisters and parents, circa 1960s.

Courtesy of Terri Bowersock

The Bowersock family—Loretta, Dave, Scott and Terri—in the 1960s.

Courtesy of Terri Bowersock

Terri and Loretta just after Loretta's 1974 divorce in what Terri describes as her mother's "Harper Valley PTA look."

Courtesy of Terri Bowersock

Loretta loved the consignment business. Her favorite saying was, "Guess what I paid for this?" Courtesy of Terri Bowersock

Loretta and Taw after they first met in the mid-1980s.

Courtesy of Terri Bowersock

The last picture taken of the five McJilton sisters in the late 1990s. (From left to right: Darla, Kay, Loretta, Shirley and Barbara)

Courtesy of Terri Bowersock

Loretta was always glamorous and professional.

Courtesy of Terri Bowersock

Terri, Loretta and Taw celebrate Terri's Entrepreneur of the Year award in 1992.

Courtesy of Terri Bowersock

Terri, Loretta and Taw on the Alaskan cruise they took in November 2004—their last happy moments together.

Courtesy of Terri Bowersock

Taw on the Alaskan cruise.   Courtesy of Terri Bowersock

Missing poster for
Loretta.

Courtesy of Terri
Bowersock

PLEASE HELP !!!

Loretta Bowersock

Went missing Dec. 13 or 14 2004
Loretta was probably buried in the Desert the
night of Dec. 13 or the morning of Dec. 14.
A reward of $1000.00 will be paid to the person
who provides information that leads directly to
the recovery of her body.

Call The Tempe Police 480-350-8306

Psychics kept seeing blue around Loretta's secret grave. She was found behind this abandoned blue motel with its plastic, blue-suited railroad porter. You can almost hear him screaming, "Hey! She's back here."

Photo by Jana Bommersbach

After months of searching, Terri could finally kneel at her mother's grave.

Courtesy of Terri Bowersock

For thirteen months, the only markers for Loretta's grave were the cacti of the Sonoran Desert.   Courtesy of Terri Bowersock

The beautiful Casa Grande Cemetery just down the road from the desolate spot where Loretta was buried.

Photo by Jana Bommersbach

Terri opened "Terri's Still N Style," a consignment store in memory of her mother. Proceeds from Still N Style and ShopTerris.com go to charity.   Courtesy of Terri Bowersock

She thought that after all these years, after having been a "family" for so long, certainly he'd have to come clean with her. Wouldn't he remember those nice Father's Day cards she used to send him? One had told him he was "such a special dad—a teacher, a supporter, a lifelong friend." One year she'd written on a funny card, "I am truly glad you are part of my life. Thank you for all your help and love and support." OK, she didn't feel that way anymore, but she had once, and she'd find that he'd kept those cards all these years, so didn't he remember, too? He didn't.

"He started telling me the same story, and I said, 'Taw, don't tell me this story. You need to stop. They have enough evidence on you and you are going to prison for this. I need to know where she is.' And he said, 'I don't know where she is.'" She remembers how he'd looked her right in the eyes and lied. "I didn't know yet that he was a pathological liar, and they have no trouble looking you straight in the eye," she says.

She wanted them to get into her car that very moment and drive to the grave, but Taw kept saying he couldn't. Her brother Scott says he knows why Taw wouldn't give up the information on where Loretta was buried: "He believed he owned her, and he buried her feeling he had that right. He allowed no one else to have any finality."

Terri left the room feeling both angry and frustrated. She says she went home that night and cried herself to sleep.

Meanwhile, Taw was making a pest of himself at the hotel, walking the halls, hanging out in the lobby, bothering other guests, constantly calling to complain that the HBO channel wasn't working. On Monday, the hotel asked him to leave. But since police had impounded the van, he needed a ride. He called Terri. Although she'd already had the Manhattan Drive house rekeyed, she didn't know where else to take him. She drove him back to the house where he'd lived for eighteen years. Within twenty-four hours, the water was turned off because the utility bill hadn't been paid.

Taw arrived home to find a fistful of notes from the media on his front door:

> *Hi! Please call—I'd like your side of the story.*
> *Thank you, sir.*
> *Steve Krafft, TV 10.*

Or this one:

> *Mr. Benderly,*
> *Please call, or your attorney. Your side should be out there too.*
> *Regards,*
> *Katie Nelson,* Republic.

Unlike Terri, who was talking to the media constantly, Taw Benderly never returned a single call or answered a single note. He had nothing to say to the media and seemed hostile that they'd taken such an interest in Loretta's "disappearance."

Terri was doing enough talking for the both of them, and not only to the press. She was also pressuring the Tempe police. She thought it was obvious

Taw was losing it, and she feared he'd run or commit suicide before ever telling where Loretta was buried. She couldn't understand how police could allow Taw to remain on his own when it seemed so clear he was on the road to self-destruction. Nor could she understand why they didn't yet have enough to hold him in custody, where his safety would be assured. She was convinced if he were pushed by police, he'd eventually buckle. He was sick, he was tired, he was scared, he couldn't hold out forever. Her only terror was that he'd kill himself first.

But police kept saying there wasn't enough evidence to arrest him; after all, there was no body, so there was no proof Loretta was dead. Even though Taw's story was in shreds, that didn't prove he'd killed her. What Terri heard was, "they were afraid to arrest him because they were afraid of lawsuits," she remembers.

Terri's friends also thought police were being too timid. "A friend offered to have people work Taw over and make him talk," Terri admits. She could easily imagine him breaking down and spilling the location of the grave if he were threatened with bodily harm. "I actually agreed, but two hours later, called him back and said, 'No, that's not right.' Thank God we didn't go through with it."

Terri called Taw every day, just to be sure he was still around. But on December 23, nobody answered the phone in the morning when she called. Nor did anyone answer when she called in the afternoon, as she and a group of friends were searching the desert. Terri called Detective Luckow with her concerns. He agreed that it didn't sound good. He met her at the

Taco Bell at Southern and McClintock to get a key to the house.

At 5:16 p.m. Tempe police "responded to Manhattan Drive to conduct a welfare check on the resident, Taw Benderly," according to the report later written by Officer Michael B. Vick.

His incident report notes:

We exited the vehicles and got into a formation, Officer Ommette carried the shield, Sergeant Papke was armed with a rifle, I carried a Taser and Officer Ribotta was armed with a handgun. We approached the resident [sic] and walked in formation to the front door. Once at the front door Sergeant Papke knocked on the door and stated, "Tempe Police, Taw we just need to talk with you" but received no response. Sergeant Papke then knocked on the door a second time and stated "We know you are in there, we just need to talk with you" but again received no response.

Police used Terri's key to unlock the front door. They announced themselves again as they entered the house in a protective formation that is drilled into officers at the police academy. The living room was empty. They went down the hall to the master bedroom. The television was on. There was a cell phone lying on the unmade bed. But no one was there. They retreated down the hall to the kitchen, checking all closets and cabinets along the way. The kitchen was empty. So was a small laundry room off the kitchen. In the laundry room was a door that led to the garage. Officer Vick reported:

The door was opened and as Officer Ommette entered the garage he advised us that he could see a subject hanging on the north east side of the garage. As we entered the garage I observed a white male subject hanging from the top of the garage. The subject had a yellow extension cord tied around his neck and his feet were just touching the garage floor. As we approached the subject, officer Ommette touched the subject and stated the subject was cold and appeared to be deceased.

Waiting outside was Taw's new attorney, Robert Baumann, who also had been unsuccessfully calling him all day. Police had called him, hoping he could get Taw to talk. "I was watching from a distance and officers came out and told me they found him," Baumann remembers. "They wouldn't tell me anything except he wasn't alive."

The media were monitoring police channels and rushed to the house when they heard officers were making a "welfare check." Terri was a half-mile away, waiting as she'd been instructed with family friend Margarita Quiauit at the Taco Bell. Finally, she couldn't wait anymore. By the time she got to the house, the media were already there. They were the ones who told her that Benderly had hanged himself. She told the media she prayed he'd left a note, because he never would tell her where he'd buried Loretta. "You look for that hope, and that hope has just been knocked out," she said. "You're looking for answers, and now the answers are gone."

Police searched the entire house, but realized that

Taw Benderly hadn't had the decency to leave a note. His final act was to leave this world with all Loretta's loved ones still in limbo, still grieving without a body to bury. Or, as Scott Bowersock put it, Taw's end was "an evil and cowardly deed."

"He didn't leave a note because he was an egomaniac," Scott adds. "He knew he'd be caught, and he saved everyone a helluva lot of trouble by hanging his ass."

But when Taw's friend Gary Bailey heard about the suicide, he had the opposite reaction: "When I found out he was found hanging, I thought, Whoever these people are, they've got Loretta and now they've hung Taw. I would never have thought he'd kill himself. It took a while for me to see what was going on. It was so tragic, I couldn't believe it was happening."

Lorraine Combs, who thought Benderly was such a nice friend, says she still can't believe it. "I'm dumfounded he didn't do more to help Terri find her mother's body."

But Dr. Pitt says it isn't hard to see that it would end up like this. "Eventually the jig is up," he says. "You can lie and lie and lie, but it's so damn hard to keep track of all your lies. It's tiring, it takes a lot of energy and eventually, it all catches up with you. He got to the point where he knew he was doomed, and he wouldn't and couldn't tolerate it."

Benderly's final acts revealed the real man, Dr. Pitt says. "He's a selfish, entitled coward. Given his personality, I would have been surprised if he'd left a note."

Police now sought yet another warrant to see what evidence Taw had left behind since returning from Tucson. While they waited, Detective Luckow reports, Terri came to him and turned over five items she'd collected as evidence as she played amateur detective. They included a set of keys to the van; a plastic Baggie containing Loretta's toothbrush, if they needed it for her DNA; a Maglite black flashlight Taw had given her "and told her to use it for her search in the desert"; a notebook with business paperwork; and two credit cards belonging to Taw.

Detective Luckow went back inside to help gather evidence. In the garage, Taw Benderly was still hanging from the garage door track rail. He was wearing a gray sweatshirt, and matching sweatpants and black slippers. He wasn't wearing his glasses, which were found in the master bedroom. At midnight, two investigators from the Maricopa County Office of the Medical Examiner arrived to untie Benderly and take his body for an autopsy. They found no evidence of foul play and concluded Taw had taken his own life.

As officers searched the garage they found what became Evidence Item No. 133: "a large map which included an area of Arizona along Interstate 8 and Stanfield Road." As Luckow pointed out in his report:

I noted that Stanfield Rd. was a location and exit east of the junction of I-8 and Hwy 84, where the cell tower was used in order for cell calls to be made on 12/13/04 by

*Benderly. In an area on the map noted as the Tohono
O'odham Indian Reservation, there appeared to be a site
marked by hand in ink along a gas pipeline.*

Police would later search along this pipeline,
and although they were close, they never found
Loretta.

The next week, Detective Luckow went back to
Baumann, hoping Taw had told him something he
could now share with police, since the attorney-
client privilege no longer applied. Unfortunately, except for relating that Taw had claimed to be Loretta's
"heir," there wasn't anything.

As Loretta's sister Barbara Fabic wrote to the
Tucson Police Department in a thank-you letter on
December 27, 2004: "Taw was always an enigma,
and he remains so in death."

The letter began:

*We, Loretta Bowersock's sisters and families, are grate-
ful to Detective Pacheco, Ralph Taylor, Dan Phillpelli,
Kevin Lane, Officer Aimmerling, and other officers who investigated Loretta's disappearance. My nephew, Matt Neal
of the Hutchinson, Kansas Police told us from the beginning
that the Tucson police department is highly respected in police circles as being very able and professional. From what
my [family] tells me, you have also been keenly aware of the
personal agony of family members. Loretta is/was an as-
sertive, healthy woman who, despite her age, would not be
an abductible person.*

*Our family members have always been uneasy about
the fact that we knew nothing of his family or background
prior to his meeting Loretta. . . . I used to think of him as*

a modern-day Mr. Micawber, Charles Dickens' famous character who always had great 'prospects' that never panned out. Taw was, unfortunately, a more sinister and larcenous version of Micawber.

CHAPTER 10

The Horrible Discoveries

Terri held her breath as she walked into her mother's house. It looked as it always had, spotless and neat, with so many wonderful "finds" filling the rooms. Here was a figurine from a yard sale where the people clearly didn't realize what a gem they had. There was a chair from a moving sale, and a lamp that had come into the consignment store. She could see her mother with each piece; remember her joy at finding such deals. These possessions all sat there, as they always had, as though nothing unusual had happened in the last nine days—oh God, was it only nine days since this nightmare had begun?

Nothing in this house even hinted that two people had died here: one whose life was taken, the other whose life was given away.

And so she held her breath, amazed that it didn't look different, didn't smell different. It was just her mother's house, but her mother wasn't here anymore.

Terri remembers crying softly as she started wandering through the rooms where her mother and Taw had lived. The dining room brought back so many memories of family dinners—all the china and silver were still in their place. The kitchen was hardest, because this is where everyone "hung out" when it was a short visit, Loretta drinking tea, Terri drinking cranberry juice. She avoided the bedroom altogether, but went into the offices—her mother's orderly; Taw's, the clutter her mother always hated

Terri had never spent much time in this room, so it felt the safest; there weren't treasured memories to come flooding in as she sat in her mother's swivel chair at the desk that looked prepared for a day's work. Taw's desk didn't share that neatness.

And then she started opening drawers and sliding back the doors of closets, and eventually she got to boxes stashed in the garage—and what she found was one shock after another.

In her wildest dreams, she'd never have expected this. Even her aunts, who'd seen Taw as a phony from day 1, had never expected this. The depth of his deceit—the immensity of his treachery—hit Terri squarely between the eyes.

"He stole my mother's identity again and again," she says, finding that he'd fill out credit-card offers, and then run up the limit, pocketing the money and never paying the bill, but going on to the next. She found at least seven cards, each one maxed out to $25,000 to $30,000.

She found the "boxes and boxes" of mail that Taw had volunteered to oversee, using the situation to scam her mother about the mortgage for so long.

She found her mother had given Taw her power of attorney, and he'd made himself the broker for her IRA—taking all that money meant for retirement out of legitimate investments and putting it into his own

company, pocketing every cent. Terri is quite sure
Loretta never knew this.

And most heartbreaking of all, she discovered the
joyful $69,000 Loretta had earned from the sale of
the house a week before her murder was now all
gone. The last $20,000 was the cash Taw had carried
to Tucson, and then passed off as a repayment to
Terri when police wanted to know why he had so
much moola on him. Terri prays to this day that
Loretta never knew.

All this was on *top* of the thousands Taw was
mooching from Terri every year. For a long time, she
couldn't figure out where all that money had gone.
She surmises Taw gave some of it to Loretta to run
the household, passing it off as "earnings" from his
inventions. But when Terri found her mother's journals and read the breathtaking anguish of her constant money concerns, she realized that if he had
given some to Loretta, he hadn't given her much.

A partial answer came as she went through the
mountains of papers she found in the house. Some of
that money had gone to pay lawyers and settle lawsuits.

Terri wasn't even shocked when she found out
Taw had been sued for defrauding investors—she'd
expected that. What she didn't know is that he'd filed
personal and corporate bankruptcy in 1992 to avoid
repayment of one judgment. Then, in a 1995 case,
there was another $58,000 judgment for fraud. But
none of the money had gone to pay this. "I don't
think we ever saw a nickel," says attorney John Fitz-
patrick, who represented the cheated investor. "I

don't think Benderly even responded to the judgment or our demand letters." He says his client finally just gave up.

But that wasn't the end of it. Loretta and Taw's company, TLC Estate Sales, also had been sued for defrauding customers. At one point, there was a $99,000 judgment against them, and a lien had been placed on Loretta's Manhattan Drive home. Loretta wrote a personal $10,310 check in 2002 to settle that case and free up the title on her house. "My mother hated being in debt, and was very conscientious about paying her bills," Terri says, and is backed up by her aunts. "This had to humiliate her."

Terri also found evidence that her mother's suspicions had led to some secret detective work over the years, and seeing that sent chills down her spine—Loretta wouldn't listen to anyone's concerns that this man was a fraud, not from her daughter, not from her sisters, not from her friends. But her own investigations told her that Taw was lying and cheating.

Loretta had tried to verify Taw's background, but her handwritten list showed that it hadn't checked out. There was "no record" that Taw had ever attended the Wharton School of Business as a classmate of Donald Trump's, Loretta wrote. There was "no record" of *any* degree, either the BA or MBA he claimed. In fact, Taw Benderly had never attended college.

She'd written that she "cannot verify" Taw's employment with one firm and "no employment confirmation" on another. "Like Taw, spring from the earth and never existed," she said of one of his claims. And she ended the note with "Because of lack of information, it is good to have antenna up."

There is no date on the list, so it's impossible to tell if she'd found out this information early in their relationship or if she'd decided to go snooping in the last couple of months. But she'd known.

Others had seen through him more easily. "I always thought there was something screwy about him, but I found him amusing—he was largely BS, but it was entertaining BS," says Craig Marks, former director of the Arizona Energy Office. "Taw was involved in a number of schemes and he had several projects he was trying to develop. He came by periodically and I met with him ten or twelve times—we had lunch more than once—but he was always lacking financial support to get these ideas going."

Marks found Taw "very full of himself" and remembers that he claimed to be the "Arizona front man" for Duke Solar and an associate of Dr. Carl N. Hodges from the University of Arizona, who was developing a system to grow plants in saltwater.

Both claims were overblown. Gary Bailey was with Duke Solar then—the company has since merged with another—and was a personal friend of Taw's, but he never paid him a cent to "front" for Duke. "I know he used that claim, and I warned him about it. I told him, 'You can't say you're our representative,'" Bailey remembers. "Taw would make claims that weren't realistic, and I'd come behind him and have to clean it up—you do that a couple times and you lose all credibility, and people don't want to do business with you," he says. He remembers Taw organizing a meeting over a potential solar energy plant for the diamond mines of South Africa, but promising things that were impossible. Those people told Bailey they wanted to work with his company, but wanted nothing to do with Taw.

Bailey remembers one night being alone with Loretta after the two couples had had dinner at the Tempe house and she complained, "I get so frustrated with him—he wants to show off, but nothing ever happens." Bailey had to admit that that surprised and dismayed him, too.

Dr. Carl N. Hodges, founder of the Seawater Foundation, which is indeed developing a new salt-water system that "will provide the planet with the first new agriculture in 10,000 years," says he can't remember Taw Benderly. His office did find a file on Benderly that showed the two men had met at least twice, but everything was a "lick and a promise"—idea meetings, nothing of substance.

But while Loretta had known that his professional background was phony, it appears she never knew Taw had also lied about his entire personal history. Terri wouldn't know any of that either, until people started calling to tell her that Taw Benderly had ruined their lives, too.

While Taw told Loretta he'd never been married—passing himself off as a widower to the Tucson police—neither was true. He had been married twice before—both women were still alive. He had two natural children whom he'd abandoned when they were small, and two stepchildren. He'd ripped off both women, mortgaging off the family home from one, stealing the daughter's college fund from the other. He'd simply walked away from each of them and disappeared. Terri says she can't count the number of times she wishes he'd taken that way out this time, too.

And Taw Benderly wasn't an orphan raised by a grandmother with no family. He was a son and a brother, and his family nickname was "Bup." Terri was told by Taw's family members that he was a messed-up child, and she always wondered if that led him to become an abuser.

She will never forget the day in 2005 when she received Ben Benderly's anguished letter.

Dear Terri:

It is a sad state of affairs when a talented fellow, my son Taw, should wind up his life in such a mixed up manner and to have all those who cared for him puzzled as to why.

Twenty-five years ago, he managed to lose touch with all those who cared for him. His father, mother, brother and son and daughter did not hear a word from him until your mother disappeared and he committed suicide. . . .

Ben's voice is old and shaky over the phone, and you sense there's pain in his heart when he hears his son's name. "He was a stranger to me for thirty years," Ben Benderly says. "He walked away from the whole family. I have no idea why, but we accepted the fact this is what he wanted. Some of these things, you have no control over." He asks that the questions stop, and that's all he wants to say, and there isn't another thing a decent human being would ask this man, who still can't understand what happened to the boy he'd unconventionally christened "Taw," just because "I liked the name."

Taw's brother, Jason, says it's "completely" incomprehensible that he could have killed someone. "I don't know anything about his life over the last twenty years except what I know from Terri," he says, then begs off from saying more.

His aunt, Virginia, says, "I haven't seen Taw since he was a young man, but I don't want to say anything that would hurt Ben. I don't want to put him through more." But she told the *Arizona Republic* that Taw had come from a wealthy East Coast family, and that his grandfather Solomon Benderly had helped create programs for Jewish children in New York.

His stepdaughter, Kristen Hays, says she learned about his suicide and Loretta's death when Taw's first wife called with the news. Kristen said she'd gone online to read the stories out of Arizona detailing the crime.

"This is one situation he couldn't lie his way out of," she surmises. "He was sixty-seven and had run out of stories."

Taw had spent six years in her family's life, and there was "a lot of conning and subterfuge, but never as far as his first wife or Loretta," Kristen says. The only flash of physical anger she ever saw from him was one day when she was about 15 and they were home alone and got into a fight. "He made a motion like he was going to backhand me. I jutted out my chin and said, 'Go ahead, you do and you're out of here,' and he backed off, because he knew I was right." After he'd left them, Hays' family discovered he had taken about $3,000 of Kristen's college savings account, had taken out loans against their house and borrowed on their glass collection.

The horrible discoveries extended into Terri's own family, as her aunts and her mother's friends finally ponied up the kind of information you don't normally tell a daughter—except under these circumstances.

Aunt Darla Neal from Kansas—the daughter praised as the "family organizer" at her mother's funeral—revealed how all the sisters had thought he was a leech. She clearly resents that a lot of people thought Taw had "conned" everyone. "Not in our family," she says. "We believed him to be phony from the beginning. There is no question in my mind that he was a sociopath. He tried very hard to be one of the group and fit in, but he had no feel whatsoever of how to do it. It was all directed from the intellect with no genuineness or sincerity attached."

Some of the sisters had even greater fears, like Kay, the one remembered as "everyone's touchstone." As Neal reports, Kay had so feared Taw that from the time she met him until she died on New Year's Eve of 2000, "she watched every episode of *America's Most Wanted*—she was sure she would see him on the show one day."

For Darla, her "bullshit meter" never turned off. "I didn't know what he was, but I knew he wasn't what he said he was. He annoyed us—he crowded us. He was too in-your-face. He was very polite, saying all the right things to be gracious, but it was like pretending to be something he wasn't."

Like everyone who knew him, she remembers how he "knew everything about everything." Although he claimed not to have children, "he knew everything about raising kids," Darla remembers. Although he claimed to have been an alternative to the U.S. Ski Team, he couldn't remember where the Olympics were staged that year—a dubious memory loss, at best.

Taw wanted to be respected as smart, accomplished and sophisticated.

But his baloney was so notorious, even the teenagers in the family made fun of him behind his back. Darla's 15-year-old son Matthew once joked that he had the perfect Halloween costume for Taw: "He should wear a black turtleneck and go as a ballpoint pen—he's done everything else."

Darla remembers how "helpful" Taw offered to be as the girls' mother was failing—he was so good at finance, he said, that he offered to take over her mother's banking. "Loretta thought it was a good idea," Darla remembers, "but the rest of us said, 'Not only no, but hell no.'"

She remembers the last New Year's Eve of Loretta's life, when she'd told Darla that her resolution "was to listen to the taps on her shoulder"—her inner conscience warning her of danger. As Darla says, "There were lots and lots of taps that this thing with Taw was wrong." She wishes her sister had followed through with that resolution.

But her biggest regret is this one: "One time Loretta asked me, 'How do you de-escalate issues? Loretta was fairly hot-tempered, and I was never sure what she was saying to me. Was she talking about de-escalating her behavior or his? Why didn't I ask? Didn't I want to know? I've questioned myself a lot why I didn't pick up on that." She fears now that her sister was trying to tell her that Taw had gotten physically abusive.

"Yes we tried to make Loretta see, but we didn't try hard," Darla says. "Our family believes in 'peace at all cost,' but we've learned that is very expensive. I don't recommend it anymore. We've felt a lot of responsibility for not making her more aware." Her oldest sister, Barbara—labeled the "scholar, teacher, keeper of the family tree"—had once offered a drastic solution: "We could have hired a hit man to kill him, and we'd all be in prison now talking about it."

Aunt Shirley Gates in Colorado—the one known for her "great humor"—says that Loretta and Taw stayed with them six to eight times in 2004, while Taw was working on "a big deal. Yeah, all he was doing was visiting us." She remembers asking her one day, when she was alone with Loretta in the car, "Why is this deal going to go when none of the others have?" and Loretta just responded, "I don't know." Shirley admits "that's as much as I wanted to confront her. Whenever we tried, she'd say, 'It's my life.' "

Shirley has an if-I'd-just-thought-of-that regret: "Loretta watched Dr. Phil every day. Why didn't I use his line on her? 'And how's that workin' for you?' He also says, 'Past behavior is the best indicator of future behavior,' and that fit Taw to a *T*. I wish I'd reminded Loretta of that."

But the worst fear the sisters had was not that Loretta would end up dead—"We'd given up the idea he was an axe murderer," Darla says—but that one day he'd simply take all the money and leave her high and dry. What a nice alternative that would have been, they now say.

The aunts also learned about the horror story of the two "buy-outs" that ended Loretta and Terri's business partnership, and tore apart their relationship. It's not surprising that neither had ever wanted to admit to the family what had happened there. "We didn't know about that," Darla says. "It wasn't shared with us."

Terri found other secrets from her mother's friends that had never been shared either, but now, as they talked and tried to console one another, Terri was no longer the "little girl" of their friend, but her survivor.

Among the first friends Terri turned to was Joy Evans in California, a woman who considered herself Loretta's "best friend" and had gotten Loretta's "upset" call on that last Sunday. "Is my mom there?" Terri asked the first night her mother was gone. "She's missing and I thought maybe she came to you."

That's when Terri learned her mother had intended to visit Joy, but was waiting for the cheaper fourteen-day fare. Joy still feels guilty about that. "Why didn't I just buy her the ticket?" she asks, and remembers it was painful to share some of her insights into Loretta with Terri.

"I didn't like Taw from the start. I hated his guts, big time," Joy says. "He gave her this cockamamie story when he showed up, and I told her his story was bullshit and she needed to check it out," she recalls. "He couldn't look me in the eye. I had a bad feeling about him, and I'd catch him in lies, but Loretta would always excuse it."

Joy was one of the friends Loretta hoped would invest in Taw's inventions. "They had me over—she loved him and believed in him, and she was desperate," Joy says. "Desperate people do desperate things. She just wanted him to succeed so bad. So he did a presentation and asked if I'd want to invest. I said no. And he asked if I didn't want to invest even a little amount. I said no again, and they never asked me again."

Eventually, Loretta was honest with Joy about how things were falling apart. "After about ten years, Loretta told me she was disillusioned, and said, "He's not pulling his weight,' and I said, 'If he has all this knowledge, why isn't he working for a corporation?' Loretta said, 'He wants to work for himself,' and I answered, 'That's fine, but people need to make a living.' Loretta said she gave him a year to bring in money, and two years later, when it was clear that still wasn't happening, I asked her what was going on. 'I've made my bed and have to lie in it,' she told me, and I told her, 'No you don't. You can move here with me.' But she never did."

Joy is convinced that at the end—in the moments before he strangled her—Loretta was "absolutely" throwing Taw out.

Police were hearing the same kinds of things from Loretta's closest friends in the days immediately after her "disappearance." Taw was still alive, still claiming he knew nothing and Loretta had just "gone missing" when Tempe police detective Susan Schoville conducted a long phone interview with Loretta's twenty-year friend Ursula Kramer in Vista, California.

Ursula had gotten a phone message from Loretta on that last Sunday: "Let's talk. Got lots to tell you." And she hoped it meant good news about the sale of the rental house. But Ursula had a busy schedule and didn't get a chance to return the call until Wednesday. She heard Taw's voice on Loretta's cell phone, but he was obviously talking to someone else and didn't actually speak into the phone. (Taw was being interviewed by Tucson police at that moment.) Ursula thought it was bizarre, and waited for Loretta to call her back. But by then, her friend was dead.

She told police one of her constant memories of Loretta is that "she was just, like, going crazy, because they never had any money."

"She didn't financially trust Taw," Ursula told police, "because he spent all the money all the time. . . . It just went through his fingers. And she always said that she had to control him, because he spent money all the time on crap, on junk, on a toy, electronics and things like that." She was asked if he was spending his money or Loretta's. "Her money. He never had any money," Ursula told the detective.

The other memory is how Taw and Loretta "were so connected at the hip all the time—he was always, always around. And she could never get rid of him."

The two women couldn't even talk on the phone without Taw interrupting from the background. Ursula would advise her, "Tell him to butt out," and Loretta would scream at him before the conversation could resume.

Ursula remembers asking her friend, " 'What are you doing with this loser?' As far as I'm concerned, she was just his cash cow. But this is the dichotomy: Loretta was a very strong person, she was beautiful, but she'd say, 'Well, I don't want to be alone,' and I said, 'Loretta, you're not alone. You've got me, and you've got friends.' " But Ursula knew that wasn't enough for Loretta: not being alone to her meant not being without a man.

Ursula had a couple of bizarre phone conversations with Taw after Loretta's disappearance, but he answered her frantic questions with "I don't know what happened." She told the officer she was shocked to discover the Tempe house was in foreclosure and said she is certain Loretta didn't know about it, because "she would have been so angry that she would have called and told me."

Everything was still very up-in-the-air at the moment of this interview, but Ursula was quite certain the worst had happened to her friend: "At first I thought to myself, Well, maybe she just ran off and disappeared and had her fill of Taw. But you know what? If she had ran off, she would have either gone to her sister's, or she would [have] come to me."

The information that hurt Terri the most came from one of Loretta's oldest friends—the one who had turned away because of Taw. Skyla Petersen had known Loretta for thirty-two years—for twenty of them, "we were best friends who spoke on the phone almost every day." She'll never forget that the day Billie Jean King beat Bobby Riggs in a "battle of the sexes" tennis match, she and Loretta had celebrated by challenging two men to a doubles match. The women won.

But in the mid-90s, "I walked away because I couldn't stand to see what Taw was doing to her," she says.

Skyla had been there the day Taw arrived on the motorcycle, and her antenna went up instantly at the strange story he told. She quickly saw how Loretta was taken with him. "He could be it all to her—her lover, her teacher, her best friend," she says. "He was a Svengali to her."

She watched as Taw took over Loretta's life. "He put together a schedule and mapped out her day. I knew better than to go over there at six-thirty p.m., because that was their reading time. He was a total control freak. There were definitely two Taws—one side was nice, charming and bright, but the other was a larcenous personality. I didn't like his way. I couldn't understand why he wasn't in prison for something. He was trying to rip people off and was always trying to make a fast buck—that characterizes him more than anything."

Her friend's reaction dismayed Skyla. "Loretta went along with some of his schemes, and she probably didn't even realize they were nefarious. Loretta saw the charming side of him. He was sucking her in, and that's why I walked away."

She remembers their last lunch together at the Lakes in Tempe, a housing development built around an artificial lake in the middle of the desert. By then, Skyla had been sickened by the rift Taw had engineered between Loretta and her daughter. "I was there the day they opened their first store," she says, "and Loretta was being unfair to Terri. I was watching her evolve, and I didn't like it." She says her friend changed from a self-assured, independent woman to an unsure, clinging one. "There was nothing I could do," she says. "He had her in his psychological trap. He had her captivated. And when it's a choice between a boyfriend and a girlfriend, it's going to be the boyfriend."

None of that was as devastating to Terri as what she found in her mother's personal journals. As she searched the house, she found notebook after notebook filled with her mother's handwriting, detailing the agony in the household year after year.

In the early 1990s, Loretta escaped to Skyla's home for a week, leaving behind a note for Taw:

I use to be able to do things for myself! I could crawl up on ladders and get signs down. Now Taw has to do everything for me. I could stop at my own desk and look at the mail . . . without Taw looking over my shoulder. . . . We are truly two damaged souls. I am so stressed. I badly need a vacation. I am over the Brink and I know it!!!!. I'm not healthy enough to handle my shit and yours!

If the break helped, it was a temporary reprieve. Another note sounded real alarms:

When you and I shout ugly messages to each other, I have heart palpitations and irregular heart beats that scare me and I fear either a stroke or heart attack and being a cripple and not able to be self-reliant. I am losing confidence that it will ever be different and I do not want to live like that. We are out of control and I don't want to ruin my health just to be in a relationship with you. This is unacceptable. You can't live here and yell and argue with me. Make a decision.

At one point, Loretta sat down and listed her "fear inventory." It shows a woman in a lot of pain. Num-

ber one, of course, was "fear of financial insecurity."
And then it goes on:

*Fear others taking advantage of me. Fear of being un-
deserving. Fear of lawsuits. Fear of being weak and sick
and helpless and having to depend on others to take care
of me. Fear of physical pain.*

In her journal on January 2, 1992, she wrote:

*Taw has to be right even if he knows he's not. It's his
core issue. The problem in our relationship is we can't be
equal adults.*

One letter after another spoke to all these complaints, again and again and again. Her sister Darla
says even a cursory reading of the letters tells you
there was no happiness here. "I can't read her journals, they're too painful," she admits.

But Loretta wasn't the only one who had complaints. And if anything spotlights the "two sides of
Taw" that so many of Loretta's friends and family
saw, it's the two letters he wrote her on January 30,
1991—just six years into their eighteen-year relationship.

The first letter is a classic of dominant, superior,
alpha-male Taw, who laid the blame on Loretta's
doorstep:

*I am unwilling to continue to accept all the blame for
your crisis. I am not the first person to be in an adver-
sarial position with you. . . . Can anybody live up to*

your ideals? I have my own issues with which to deal. It seems that we cannot even have the simplest conversation without ending up in a violent argument over the slightest illusion of a differing opinion or phrasing or methods. It doesn't seem to matter what the issues are, but only that there is an obvious power play taking place between us.

It is difficult for me to accept your statements of my enrichment of your life. If I perceived you as enriching in my life with the following exceptions, I would question my judgment.

1. Taw you are too controlling.

2. Taw, you enrage me with your style of speech.

3. Taw, you have put me in serious debt.

4. Taw, you brought too much baggage to our relationship.

5. Taw, you have ruined my relationship with my daughter.

6. Taw, you are obviously not trustworthy.

7. Taw, you don't bring any joy or fun into my life, only problems.

8. Taw, I don't like. . . . .

9. Taw, I don't like. . . . .

10. Taw, I don't like. . . . . and on, and on, Taw, I LOVE YOU, BUT. . . . .BUT. . . . ..BUT. . . . . BUT. . . . .

If I perceived you, Loretta, as you appear to perceive me, I would run you out of my life fast, faster, fastest.

The second letter, dated 11:35 p.m., takes an entirely different tone. This letter feels like a petting, reflecting the charming, suave, loving, vulnerable Taw who had first appealed to Loretta:

My response was selfish and based on fear. The fear of losing you, not just the fear of abandonment. I cannot lose what I don't own. I don't own you or your love. Your love can only be a gift to me, and I can't lose a gift. I can throw it away or discard it, but I can't lose it.

I don't know if I can continue to risk my emotional sense of self in a relationship with you. I think I am willing to take some additional risks, but I am afraid. It is very difficult for me to give up the control of all that occurs around me, even if that control is just illusionary.

I want a relationship with you. I need love, care, tenderness and understanding from my significant other. I expect to have my expressed wants and needs acknowledged, validated and as many as possible, met. . . .

I think you are a wonderful woman, sensuous, sexy, smart, capable and caring. I see that you have issues of your own to solve. You will be that much more desirable to me when you have successfully dealt with them.

I close with a prayer: May our spiritual guide help us in our quest for peace, joy, tranquility and prosperity, each of us and we together . . . forever.

My love and affection,
Taw.

And so their lives went on for eighteen years: trauma, reconciliation, fights, make-ups, fears, hopes, tears.

If Taw was on a personal search for understanding, he put almost nothing on paper. The few things he did—apparently in prodding from Loretta in her self-help quest—reflect a man who thinks he's perfectly fine, just not getting his needs met.

Loretta was never so kind to herself. Perhaps the most heartbreaking list she ever made was her list of "forgiveness." One of her self-help classes told her to give herself forgiveness for her own failings, so she wrote them out:

I forgive myself for not being "enough" to attract a kind, gentle, supportive, secure, honest, financially viable man as a partner.

I forgive myself for recreating my childhood in a family where my Dad didn't adequately provide for us and recreating it with Taw.

I forgive myself for being a rescuer and deceiving myself that I am a partner building a future.

I forgive myself for accepting so little for so much of me.

CHAPTER 11

The Media

The minute Loretta Bowersock's disappearance hit the Channel 5 newsroom in Phoenix, Donna Rossi wasn't sure which of her connections kicked in first: her old days as a Phoenix cop, her eighteen years as an Arizona journalist or her friendship with Terri Bowersock. "But I immediately thought, Everybody knows Terri, this is going to be big."

She knew she'd want the first interview with Terri—that was the journalist in her; she already suspected the worst—the cop talking—and she knew Terri would know how to work the media.

"You do think, Oh my God, somebody I know is affected by the stuff I cover every day," Rossi says. "There are some people in Arizona that are a media phenomenon—Sheriff Joe is like that. He can burp and get coverage." [She's talking about the man who likes to call himself "the world's toughest sheriff" and is both loved and loathed in Arizona.] "On a smaller scale, Terri is a lot like that. She single-handedly kept that story alive in the media, and she used her business and PR savvy to make this work for her, and she did that in the middle of her grief."

Rossi did get one of the first interviews, and then

an interview with Terri about her mother's disappearance became the easiest "get" in Arizona journalism: "She made herself available to everyone, and she let us talk to anyone," Rossi says. "I have never dealt with a victim more conscious of my deadlines than Terri Bowersock. She knew the news cycle. She knew that Saturdays are a 'slow news day' and so, on Thursday or Friday, we'd get notified that Terri was going out to search the desert on Saturday, and every news organization would be out there. It was a great move."

It didn't hurt that Terri knows a good quote when she speaks it.

The first words in the first major story printed by the *Arizona Republic*, were these:

"Mom, I'm gonna find you; Mom, I'm gonna find you."

Katie Nelson's first story—she'd go on to write eighteen—continues:

So goes Terri Bowersock's tearful message to her missing 69-year-old mother.

Loretta Bowersock disappeared in Tucson on Tuesday while she and her husband were visiting there this week. The couple live in Tempe, where her daughter also runs a multimillion-dollar chain of consignment stores, Terri's Consign & Design Furnishings Inc. . . . Police are treating the disappearance as a missing person case but are investigating for possible foul play.

"It's scary, first and foremost, it's scary," Terri said while stopping by her mother's Tempe home accompanied by co-workers. "Your thoughts can get away from you." . . . She said she had not slept in days. "I keep a phone with me

and keep moving," she said. "I stay wherever I can help."
Benderly is still in Tucson. His stepdaughter said he was
"shook up and trying to process everything."

The strain on the family was clear Thursday morning,
when Terri returned to Tempe. She is media savvy, often ap-
pearing on news shows and in magazines or in ads for her
nine stores. But while her demeanor was calm in front of
cameras, Terri's voice broke and she took a deep breath be-
fore pleading into news cameras for information about her
mother: "Please keep an eye out there, and they'll keep
looking in Tucson. Thanks to everybody for your support
and love. We'll find her."

Terri's first news conference, three days after her
mother went missing, again showcased her quotabil-
ity. She told the press that either Taw was lying or her
mother never made it inside the Dillard's store in Tucson:

"She went there to go shopping, but there's no record
of her buying anything, and at seventy-five percent off, my
mother would have bought something, I'm telling you."

Or, as she kept the media updated on police interest in Taw:

"They're questioning him a lot more. Because of the
fact that he was the last person to see her, police haven't
ruled out anything. They haven't ruled out missing,
haven't ruled out him, haven't ruled out foul play."

Or, as she declared with words that could have
come from any loving daughter:

"My mother was a beautiful, classy lady. She would not want to be left alone out in the desert."

The story originated out of Tucson, of course, since that's where Loretta supposedly disappeared, and the very first words about this case signaled great alarm: David Teibel of the *Tucson Citizen* wrote,

Police are concerned Bowersock may have fallen victim to foul play . . . "This is a lady who is very, very structured and organized," Sgt. Carlos Valdez said. Family members have told police "this is very, very, very outside her normal behavior."

The next day's story noted that most missing persons reports wouldn't be getting any media attention, but this one was hot throughout Arizona:

One of the reasons this case is getting so much attention is because of Loretta's daughter. Terri Bowersock is a well known Phoenix area businesswoman and the owner of Terri's Consign and Design, a business she started with help from her mother and grandmother.

The first report on Phoenix's Channel 3 had anchor Patti Kirkpatrick telling the city, "The mother of a well-known Valley woman is missing tonight." Then over replays of television commercials starring Terri and her mom, she gave the few details that were coming in—Loretta was missing, Tempe police were searching the garbage cans around her house, Terri was distraught and in Tucson. A police officer from

Tucson was saying into the camera, "even the smallest detail from the public could bring her home safely."

In another report, Channel 3 put it like this: "Domestic Diva Terry Bowersock is appealing to Arizonans' hearts this time, not their wallets. She wants to find her mother." Then there was a sound bite from Terri: "I have just one goal—to get my mom back," and she barely gets the words out when her voice cracks. Then she looks right in the camera and promises she won't go away, saying, "So the reason you see me all the time is, I'm a powerhouse. And I won't stop looking under every rock until I find her."

The media constantly broadcast and printed pictures of both Loretta and Taw, hoping someone would recognize one of them, and ran phone numbers for the police in case anyone had any information. When one picture had run for a few days, Terri delivered a new one to television stations and newspapers, knowing they were always looking for "fresh stuff."

For the first ten days there was a daily focus on the missing Loretta, suspicious but too-distraught-to-talk Taw and the growing realization that Loretta wasn't missing at all, but was dead and buried somewhere. The media assumed she was dead when she hadn't shown up within a day or two—but the cynical media normally go to the darkest side of any story, so that wasn't unusual. They didn't realize that many people who knew this couple—their attorney, Loretta's sisters, business associates of Taw's—had immediately suspected that she was dead, and that he had killed her.

"Few clues revealed on missing woman," was a

story in the *East Valley Tribune* by Kristina Davis on December 18:

Terri Bowersock feels like she's running out of time. It's been four days since anyone has heard from or seen her mother . . . and police have released no clues in the investigation.

"I feel very strongly that something happened to her," the 48-year-old owner of Terri's Consign and Design Furnishings said Friday. "I feel like I have a very small window now to find her. It's important for me to do everything I can right now. I don't think I've let myself stop looking." Missing posters have been posted in her furniture stores across the Valley and in Tucson . . . and friends and family plan to hand out more.

The case was turned over to the Tempe Police Department on December 21, and Sergeant Dan Masters began issuing regular press releases and updates on the case to help satisfy the media attention. The first one read:

For the last week, detectives from the Tempe and Tucson Police Departments have been working together on this case. At this time, police have not been able to corroborate Mr. Benderly's story that he dropped-off Ms. Bowersock at a Tucson Mall. Her last known and confirmed whereabouts is in Tempe, last Monday, December 13. In light of this, it is appropriate for our department to commence our own investigation.

A team of detectives from our missing persons/homicide detail are currently assigned to this case. They are meticulously examining the facts and circumstances of her disappearance and will actively pursue all leads which develop. We are also working closely with Terri Bowersock, the victim's daughter.

Mr. Benderly is considered an investigative lead in her disappearance. We believe he has information that would be beneficial in helping us solve this case. Although he provided Tucson Police with an initial interview/statement, he has since refused to answer any further questions by police. He is not in police custody. We encourage anyone with information regarding this case to contact the Tempe Police Department.

As Sergeant Masters elaborated on Benderly in press interviews, "Undoubtedly, he holds all of the answers to most of the questions we have surrounding her disappearance. At this point what we have is circumstantial evidence, though. We don't have any physical, concrete, tangible evidence to establish that a crime took place yet."

In other words, nobody could prove there was a murder because there was no body. Loretta could just be missing and not dead. Maybe she just ran away. It sure didn't look like that, but what they had so far wasn't enough to lay a murder charge on anyone.

But Sergeant Masters held out hope: "We're confident that in time and hopefully sooner, rather than later, all our *i*'s will be dotted and our *t*'s crossed."

But whatever *i*'s and *t*'s were being completed inside the police department, not much new was being released to a media that doesn't dwell long on stories that go stale. "Still No Sign of Missing Woman," headlines started saying. "Mother of Valley Business Woman Remains Missing"; "Few Clues Revealed on Missing Woman."

"Missing Woman's Daughter Consults Psychic," one headline read—this angle of the story didn't get much play, as many media outlets treat psychic involvement like voodoo nonsense.

Neither the Tucson Police Department nor the Pima County Sheriff's Department hire psychics to assist in their investigations, but Loretta Bowersock's daughter has been in contact with one. "One of the things psychics are looking for," says Terri Bowersock, "is clothing, so I went home to get robes, a pillowcase, and jewelry so these were all things she wore and for psychics, they need content."

One week after Loretta's disappearance, the *Republic* ran another Katie Nelson story:

It has been a week since Tempe resident Loretta Bowersock disappeared. That thought is painful for her daughter, Terri, who acknowledges that her 69-year-old mother may be dead. But Terri continues to search, with the help of her Terri's Consign & Design employees and the police. And she will take solace in what is in front of her.

Things like two gold, diamond-studded rings her mother wore almost daily. That jewelry is on Terri's hands now as she walks the desert accompanied by a psychic and a half-dozen of her friends.

And then Taw committed suicide. Or did he?
The cynical media immediately asked themselves

if this pathetic guy had offed himself, or if the grieving daughter had helped.

"For a second you had to think—did Terri lose it
and kill him?" Donna Rossi of Channel 5 recalls. "If
you didn't think that, you wouldn't be doing your job
as a journalist. You have to think outside the box. Anybody is capable of murder in the right circumstances.
But I knew Terri, and I knew she's a very spiritual person. While she may have wanted to beat the information out of him, killing him is a tall order."

The media didn't know Terri's friends had offered
to rough him up, and that she'd agreed, but then
called them off. "Just imagine if we'd gone through
with it, and they'd found him with bruises," Terri says
with a shudder. "They'd have thought we murdered
him. Wouldn't that have been a kick in the head?"

Even without knowing about the aborted roughing
up, police naturally investigated Taw's death to determine whether it truly was a suicide. The day after,
Tucson detective John McGowan petitioned the
court for another search warrant of the Manhattan
Drive house. It now potentially held clues in two
deaths. He specifically asked for:

—*Trace evidence including but not limited to blood,
hair fibers and DNA evidence.*
—*Items used in the strangulation of the [sic] Taw Benderly to include but not limited to an extension cord and
towels.*
—*Any items of clothing which may contain biological
or trace evidence or damage to the clothing indicating the
crime may have occurred.*

—*Mail in mailbox.*

—*Access to review and record from any cell phones or other recording devises that may contain information leading to the location of the victim [Loretta] or other evidentiary value indicating the crime may have occurred.*

—*Phone records that document numbers called and in particular any recorded long distance numbers.*

—*Any paper receipts indicating purchases or payments which may indicate locations and dates related to the crime.*

—*Any garden type tools or digging type tools.*

As Detective McGowan told Maricopa County superior court judge Jay L. Davis, "Your affiant believes a check of the residence for the listed items would aid in the location of Loretta Bowersock and assist in the death investigation of Taw Benderly." The judge issued the warrant that day.

Tempe homicide detective Trent Luckow just laughs when he's asked if he's sure Taw committed suicide: "It was definitely obvious that this was self-inflicted."

The suicide itself wasn't the focus of most of the news reports—everybody pretty much had decided this guy was guilty of murder; taking his own life seemed almost anti-climactic—no, the big news was the question: Did he leave a note?

On television, Terri is shown saying, "I'm just real shook up, I don't know what to think right now. I want to know if there is a note. I just hope he loved her enough that he left a note for her or me. Because my mom doesn't deserve this."

She told the *Republic*, "You look for that hope,

and that hope was just knocked out. You're looking for answers, and now those answers are gone."

Sergeant Masters told Phoenix Channel 15, "They've been flipping through every page in every book on every shelf looking for a note."

A couple of news and Internet outlets reported there was a note.

A one-sentence message, typed on a new laptop Taw had bought since returning from Tucson, was the best anyone got. At 1:37 p.m. on December 18, he had sat down and created a file named "Vows for Eternity." The entire file contained only this one sentence that he hadn't gone back to read since that day:

Loretta and I vowed over the years that we would spend eternity together, and so we shall.

Terri had already seen that message when she'd gotten the briefcase from Taw at the Phoenix hotel. She had tried to convince police that those words meant Taw had intended to take his own life, and she was right. But being right was little consolation when the man hadn't had the decency to set things right as he checked out. Police searched for hours, but could find nothing else. It was the final insult, and the last freaky exercise of control, of Taw Benderly's life.

Kristina Davis of the *Tribune* wrote:

Taw Benderly's suicide note revealed no secrets. The unsigned, typed note in cursive font was found in a briefcase [along with a list of items he was leaving to Terri]. The me-

mentos are the last known link to the disappearance of Loretta Bowersock, forcing her family to agonize that any clues to her fate died with Benderly, the last known person to see her alive. "He controlled a lot about her, and she fought along the way. And he has control in her death, to know where she is and have no one else know," a frustrated Terri Bowersock said.

The note indicates Benderly knew Loretta Bowersock was dead, she said, confirming why police narrowed their investigation to him days before he killed himself. "Him killing himself is very selfish for him to do that and not give us the opportunity to find her and give her a decent burial," said Loretta Bowersock's sister, Darla Neal of Hutchinson, Kan.

Channel 3's report on the suicide opened with Terri in the garage, showing how Taw had thrown an extension cord over the beam and jumped off a white wooden footstool. It's such an ordinary-looking garage—a long-handled tree clipper hangs on the wall. A tool box sits on a work bench, open, cluttered and overflowing. Two fire extinguishers are nearby; underneath are two blue boxes to hold nuts and screws. There are six white file boxes.

Terri told the camera: "When they started accusing him, he said, 'Because of that Scott Peterson guy, now they think I did that.' That's when he started crying. The first time he cried. What I believe truly happened is, he choked her. He was a very clean man, and choking is clean."

The report included a sound bite from Tempe Sergeant Dan Masters: "Mr. Benderly was leading a double life, and he fooled several people for decades.

I think his past finally caught up with him, and when confronted, he probably killed Loretta."

If police knew, or suspected all that, why didn't they arrest him—as Terri had kept pleading—so he'd be kept safely locked up, rather than leaving him on his own where he could escape in his own way?

TV reporter Carey Peña asked just that: "Some might wonder with all this evidence why they did not make an arrest," she ended her report. "They were consulting with the county attorney's office, and all this just added up to circumstantial evidence. It was not enough to constitute an arrest, not enough to believe Loretta Bowersock had been murdered. At this point, she's still considered a missing person."

The broadcast went back to the newsroom where anchor Mike Chamberlin exclaimed, "This is like a novel. It's almost like a *Monday Night Movie*. It's so multi-layered, and it's just unbelievable."

Meanwhile, the Associated Press had picked up the story, and Loretta's disappearance and the mystery surrounding her whereabouts was read throughout the country. Back in Hutchinson, Kansas, there was a "local angle" for the national story, and the *Hutchinson News* focused on her prominent sister, Darla, who was a long-time member of the Hutchinson Board of Education and the current chairwoman of the Hutchinson County Foundation. On December 23—the day Taw's body would later be found—the paper reported:

Hutchinson resident Darla Neal has given up hope that her missing sister will be found alive. Neal's wish is that

*her sister's body will be discovered as soon as possible,
perhaps somewhere in the desert near her home. "We're
concerned about finding her so we can give her a decent
burial," Neal said. Neal is convinced her sister was murdered. . . . On Wednesday while she waited for a call from
Sen. Pat Robert's office in Washington, D.C. to perhaps
learn more details of the case, Neal remembered the days
when she and her four sisters grew up together in Newton
as the five McJilton girls.*

*"You never think that something like this would happen
to someone you love," Neal said.*

In newsrooms around Arizona, this story was now
at a standstill. As Terri had said herself, "all the answers are gone." The only way to keep this story
alive—the only thing yet to resolve—was the missing body. And so the desert searches intensified.

Television cameras and reporters followed Terri
into the desert, with her pleas for help. And nobody
could watch those reports—always including a
sweeping view of the vast, harsh desert that sur-
rounds the Valley—and not feel sick to their stomachs that poor Loretta would never be found.

Valley media had something new to report as December ended and Terri held a memorial for her
missing mother at her corporate headquarters on December 29. Her aunts came to town—flying in from
Kansas, Colorado and Maryland—to join about 100
family friends, business associates and neighbors.

The memorial was one day before her brother
Scott's 50th birthday. He couldn't come from
Hawaii, but sent a private email that the media never
saw. It shows that good quotes run in the family:

*Taw had better hope that simplistic ode to eternal to-
getherness is not what happens after death. Besides waiting
for him with a frying pan, my mother would make his eternity a hell if she had to be with that man who took so much
from her.*

Terri acknowledged that some would say it was
too early to hold a memorial. "But I wouldn't be doing this if I had a doubt in my mind," she told the
crowd. "Tonight we're here for closure in our own
heart. We need to let her know we're OK, so she can
move on, too."

As Nelson reported in the *Republic*'s coverage of
the memorial.

*Loretta Bowersock was remembered as quick and fast
at the jitterbug, a gracious hostess and a cheerleader both
in practice and in life.*

There were laughs and tears as the crowd looked at
black-and-white pictures from the growing-up years
of the McJilton girls—those "high hair" days when
Loretta was the best dancer in town. "We've come
here together to mourn the loss of our sister, mother
and friend," Loretta's sister Shirley Gates said
through her tears. "Our hope is that she is at peace."

But in a newspaper world, where the emphasis is
on "new," and a television world, where the attention span doesn't extend much beyond two minutes
anyway, this story was about over. As one Channel
3 producer confided, "She's missing, she's missing, she's missing, yeah, we got it already." Without some fresh development there just wasn't any

action for television to report. How many times can you tell the same story?

That Terri had kept the coverage going so long is proof of her media savvy, but also a nod to how many journalists who'd known her over the years had gone the extra mile to keep the tired story alive. Or, like Rossi, how many could feel a personal tug. "Having already lost my mom, you can so empathize with the grief," Rossi says. "I know how Terri feels. I do have the solace of knowing what happened to my mother—she died of cancer—but if you don't know . . ."

By early January 2005, the media went hunting for new information through the courts. KPNX-TV and the First Amendment Coalition of Arizona filed a petition asking the court to "unseal" the results of the Tempe search warrants in the case. It isn't un-usual in an ongoing homicide for police to request that their search warrants remain secret to protect their evidence. But now, argued the state's top First Amendment attorney, Daniel C. Barr, with Loretta still missing and Taw dead, there was nothing left to protect. As Barr argued, Arizona's strict public records law is a "clear policy favoring disclosure of court records." The court granted the petition on January 6. The 47-page packet laid out everything police had found: the dirty pick and shovel, the suitcases full of Taw's clothing and the one satchel with Loretta's items; Loretta's black purse found in the Tempe garage; financial records, photos, a map of the desert where they thought Loretta was stashed.

"Warrant Info Sheds Light on Death Case," Nelson reported in the *Republic*, noting this was the first public information on why investigators had suspected Benderly.

She quoted Sergeant Dan Masters: "Very early on, inconsistencies in his story seemed to multiply."

But now, in fact, there wouldn't be a single new thing to report unless the body was found—and no matter how close some felt to Terri, the media had to move on. Some were more than ready. One Channel 10 reporter complained, "We never saw her grieve. We saw her trying to look good while we watched her grieve." The same reporter said there was a nagging concern that there was far more to this story than the media knew. "We kept hearing rumors about the backstory, but we never got it. We weren't even sure Terri *liked* her mother."

Eventually, even the media reported on how the media had stuck with this story because of Terri's celebrity. As Katie Nelson reported on January 7, 2005:

Terri Bowersock's business life has always kept her in the limelight.

Her face is on many of the Terri's Consign & Design Furnishings ads. She appears often on TV. The Ahwatukee woman "grew up" in the media, she said.

But as tragedy brewed last month, Terri Bowersock has caught the public's attention for a much more personal reason. Since her mother, Loretta, disappeared Dec. 14, Bowersock has appeared nearly daily on local TV, radio and newspapers, pleading for people to help find the 69-year-old Tempe woman.

"It's not that I know how to work it, it's that I'm not afraid of it," she says . . . "I've been in [the media] since we started—20–25 years. I knew that it would help."

And that was really all she had left. As Nelson reported, "Now she hopes the public spotlight will help her find her mother."

But then the TV cameras went away and even diligent Katie Nelson had other things to cover. On January 10, her headline in the *Republic* says it all: Bowersock Search Yields Nothing. Police Out of Leads in Case of Missing Tempe Woman.

The first sentence was the death knoll for the media's attention:

The last lead has evaporated.

No one was more relieved that the media had finally gone away than Tempe's lead homicide detective on the case, Trent Luckow. "This was a challenging case—it ranks right up there at the top, in my experience, and kind of mirrors the Scott Peterson case," he says. "The media involvement made it even more challenging. With Terri's attraction to the media and the media's attraction to Terri, it was challenging to keep everything in balance. When the media becomes involved, you can't necessarily focus on the case. I've got a public information officer working updates, but Terri is calling me, telling me my information officer isn't giving out enough information—we're in an up-to-the-minute society, and people want information up to date and current."

For a month in early 2005, nobody wrote a word about the missing Loretta Bowersock. Then on February 11, Terri found something new for at least one more hook. "Bowersock Creates Web Site to Aid Public—Readers can post items on dangerous people." The story reported on Terri's plan to let people vent on dangerous relatives or friends, much like folks report bad businesses to the Better Business Bureau. "It's the time now that the public informs each other instead of waiting until something tragic happens," she told the *Republic*. The Web site featured a free blog. Readers could post items about someone they felt was dangerous, and she hoped that eventually they could get a background check on a person. There was no discussion about the kind of vindictive accusations this kind of vehicle could inspire, and the whole thing eventually went away. Just like the media did.

It took two more months before Katie Nelson ran another word on the case. "Kin, Psychic Maintain Body Quest," said the April 2 story. Terri and two of her aunts had spent the day in the desert, and also posted flyers aimed at hikers and passers-by, offering a $1,000 reward.

At the one-year anniversary of Loretta's disappearance—December 14, 2005—Channel 3 came by one more time. In a lengthy report, it shows Terri saying, "I do feel her, quite a bit. I feel her presence with me." The reporter summarized the story, adding the newest wrinkle: a trucker had called to say that he'd been on a run a year ago, and seen a red van on I-8, near the area where they'd been searching all this time. But so far, they'd found nothing new.

Terri knew it was the last media present she would get. She knew nobody would come back again, because it was just the same old, same old. And she also knew that after a year of searching, there wasn't much hope anymore. She doesn't remember the day she realized she was probably never going to find Loretta, that she and her brother would spend the rest of their lives wondering where their mother's last remains lay hidden.

She wanted to believe the psychics who were still assuring her Loretta's remains would be found; she wanted to hold on to the hope that someday, she'd take Loretta's ashes to Hawaii and she and Scott would scatter them on a beach the family had once visited. But it got harder and harder to hold on to any hope.

CHAPTER 12

The Psychics

Terri Bowersock has always felt blessed that she doesn't suffer nightmares, so there was no reason to be frightened as the dream began.

She's lying on her back on the ground, holding very still, and there's sand all around her. It's pitch black, but then, the night always robs everything of color, so that was expected. There are some stars up there in the sky overhead, but they're very far away and very dim. She moves her eyes, but not her head—either she's not supposed to move or she can't move, she doesn't know which. In the darkness she can make out a shape here and there—the silhouette of a cactus nearby, something that must be a bush, a small dune right next to her. It occurs to her that there is no reason for her to be out in the desert, lying so still next to a sand dune, but it's just a passing thought. There's nothing particularly creepy about it, just strange.

And then she hears the coyotes coming. They are a ways off, but their padded paws make a distinctive sound as they hit the hard gravel of the desert floor. They are panting and sniffing, some are yelping, one lets out the howl that does its job of terrifying. It's impossible to figure out how many there are, but it's a pack and they're on their way, and then they're over the sand dune.

When a coyote nips at her fingertips, Terri wakes up screaming.

To this day, she's convinced she was experiencing a simultaneous assault on her mother's body, just three days after Loretta had gone missing. "I believe she and I connected that night," Terri says now, shuddering at the thought.

Terri has always thought of herself as "open" to the paranormal—never claiming any psychic abilities, but not ignoring the "sense" she has sometimes, either. And the dream was so incredibly real—would turn out to be so incredibly accurate—that she was convinced her mother was calling out for help.

The dream galvanized Terri into searching the desert for her mother's body, but also threw open the double doors of her heart to the psychics who came panting to this case with the same determination as those dream coyotes.

"I bet I talked to about forty psychics, and it took me a while to realize a lot of them mix up a lot of unclear messages," Terri says. "I call them 'baby psychics,' because they haven't gotten the messages clear yet. But boy, some of them really got to me."

She is very careful not to criticize those who came, offering their "visions" and their "messages" and their brand of comfort. She prefers to remember all the times somebody was right, or close enough to count, and needs to be nudged to talk about those who brought hurtful stories that only made matters worse.

"When you don't have anywhere else to turn, you

turn to whoever is there," Terri says. And for months, she felt the psychics were the only ones sticking with her. "The police gave up on this case early on," she says, "and it was left to me and my friends and the psychics to find my mother."

Police searched the desert for about a week after Loretta disappeared, but then Taw committed suicide and there was no longer anyone to prosecute for a suspected murder with no body attached to it. Some officers personally joined Terri in searching the desert—Detective Pacheco and his daughter drove up from Tucson a couple of times because he'd been so touched by Terri's need to find her mother. But as far as an official search, it seemed both pointless and futile.

Yet the psychics didn't go away. They weren't driven by the need to punish someone for a murder; they were driven by the mystery of finding a body discarded in the desert that was robbing a family of closure.

Some of them had no idea how cruel their interference in the case was.

The first to call was Angie DiMaggio of Mesa, a retired visual arts teacher who also calls herself a medium. "I'm not a sideshow, I'm very God-connected," she says. "What I got was pretty loud and clear. Loretta's spirit had been wronged, and wrongs need to be made right. She was a sweetheart lady—a good lady who trusted too much. I saw her boyfriend as someone who kept taking and taking from her until she had nothing. She went from being a smiling lady to being very, very sad."

Angie saw Loretta in a burial position with her

legs bent because the grave wasn't long enough to hold her whole body. (A vision that would prove accurate.) She called Terri to tell her about the visions and to ask for pictures of her mother. "Terri was very receptive," Angie remembers. "I've never seen a lady with such love in her heart, and determination to help her mother, no matter what she had to do. She was heartbroken, but determined to find her and help her. I don't think I would have been that strong. Terri showed amazing strength at a time of real chaos. I like Terri's tenacity and spirit, and the love she had for her mama was outstanding."

Terri would turn to Angie again and again, but her primary memory is the pain of their first meeting. "She told me Taw kicked mother and choked her and broke her leg. I almost threw up. I went home and kept seeing that."

It wasn't the last time she had to contend with ugly images. One of the early "baby psychics" called Terri just a couple of days after the coyote dream. Terri met the woman, who she won't identify, at a Village Inn restaurant. "She told me Mother had had a bad fight with Taw and was all bloody, and her leg was broken, but she saw her still alive and tied up. I went nuts." If this were true, Loretta had spent at least five days tied up and suffering in the desert.

The psychic said Loretta was to the east of Interstate 10 on the Indian reservation, and Terri called a friend who got her a helicopter. She and a couple of others went up for several hours, setting down about ten times whenever they saw anything suspicious. But there was no Loretta tied up to a tree; no sign she had ever been anywhere in this area. As it turned out, everything was wrong about this: Loretta was long dead and they were on the wrong side of the freeway. But for all those anxious hours, Terri had believed her mother was wasting away in the desert.

And then there was Rebecca Scarbrough, who brought Terri a bag of bones she'd found searching the desert for Loretta.

Rebecca doesn't consider herself a psychic. "I'm a Christian," she says. "I have a prophetic gift that allows me to see or hear things that can be helpful."

She first heard about Loretta's disappearance on the television news and felt a special link, since she knew Terri from the commercials for her consignment business. "It bothered me spiritually the minute I heard about it. I was in the living room and I looked at my mother-in-law and said, 'Oh, he killed her,'" Rebecca remembers. "The next day I had a vision, just like a cartoon. I had a picture in my brain where she was buried."

Rebecca sat down and drew a map and then called the police. She says they arranged to go up in a helicopter and spent an afternoon searching, setting down in two spots. They found the place in the vision, but Loretta wasn't there. Rebecca did pick up several bones she found at their set-down sites.

Terri remembers Rebecca showing up at her doorstep, handing her a bundle and saying, "These are your mother's bones." Rebecca maintains that she never said that, just offered the bones for whatever they could show, finding out later they were all animal bones.

But Terri remembers the moment with a special

kind of horror. She didn't get angry, she didn't react in disgust, she says she simply accepted the bones and felt sick to her stomach. But she refuses to bad-mouth Rebecca. "She thought she was helping," Terri says with generosity.

So did all those who filled Terri's mailbox for months. "People sent me maps and drawings of where they'd 'seen' my mother's grave," Terri says. She didn't dare ignore any of these messages, just in case one was the real gravesite. She can't even esti-mate how much time she wasted searching in all the wrong places.

"I had to learn how to take all this from the psy-chics and not think it was all true," she says.

Phillip Parmenter of Fountain Hills wrote offer-ing a different kind of help:

As it was recently reported that you have consulted psychics in your mother's disappearance, it became ap-parent to me that you may be open-minded to attempt what I am about to suggest. Let me begin by stating that I am not looking for any money or other reimbursement from you. My goal is paranormal research for my own in-terests, with the possibility that some clues or closure may come to you.

He then reminded her of a movie currently play-ing in theaters called *White Noise*, starring Michael Keaton. In the movie, the man is able to communi-cate with his deceased wife via Electronic Voice Phenomenon, which involves special audio and video recording techniques where noises are heard that may be communications from deceased loved ones. Terri passed on the offer.

It all got pretty wearying, and seemed as if everyone with any psychic proclivity in Arizona was adding their two cents—except the woman who was about to become the most famous psychic in the state, Allison DuBois. A television series on her life, *Medium*, was about to premiere and would go on to be a big hit.

Terri's aunt, Barbara Fabic, sought out DuBois' help. In an email on January 19, 2005, Barbara laid out the details of Loretta's disappearance and pleaded for help:

It appears that the case will be closed and searches for the body [by police] will end. Needless to say, this is devastating for us. We know that you work with authorities on cases like this. We also know that at the present time, because of national TV interviews and the launching of Medium *that you are more than unusually swamped. Channel 10 TV reporters have said that they will try to put you in touch with Terri. . . . I plead with you to contact Terri . . . We wish we had psychic powers, but we do not.*

Allison's husband, Joe, answered the email that same day:

My condolences for your loss. Yes we have heard this devastating story on the news. Allison does keep a list of cases which she is actively working on and yours has been added. The list contains over 50 cases which involve murderer's who are still at large. Allison is currently out of town promoting the new television series. Since this type of case is very draining, she can only work on it when she is in town and has the appropriate amount of time and concentration to devote. Since it will be some time until Allison can devote the necessary time to work on this, Allison has asked me to recommend someone who she has worked with before.

He gave Barbara a name and number, but nothing ever came of it.

By now, Terri was already "talking" with her mother through mediums who said they were channeling the dead woman.

Tammy Holmes is a 47-year-old Phoenix medium who says Loretta came to her. "I felt her everywhere, in the house and in my car, and she said, 'You've got to help my daughter.' I had never met Terri, I had never met Loretta, other than what I saw on television. But six to eight times Loretta came to me. I could feel and see everything. It was like watching a movie."

She called Terri with the news and Terri came running. The first time they met, Tammy told Terri how much her mother loved shopping—"anything you want is in heaven," she reported Loretta saying, and said Loretta showed up for each vision in a new outfit, "all decked out." That day, Tammy said Loretta was holding out a purse and saying, "Guess what I paid for this—on earth it would be forty-five dollars; up here, it's free." Terri remembers laughing—"Oh my God, it's her, because she did that to me all my life, playing the game of 'How much did I pay for this?' "

And then Tammy delivered the central message

she says Loretta kept repeating. "Her main concern was to heal the relationship with Terri—Loretta didn't care if we ever found the body, but she was feeling very badly about her relationship with Terri. She kept apologizing for letting Taw get between them, and she wanted Terri to know how much she loved her, how much she valued her."

Terri has total faith in Tammy Holmes and the messages she brought. "I'd see my mother's gestures in Tammy's face; I'd hear my mother in her tone," Terri says. "Tammy responded in tone and rhythm to how my mother talked. And Mother kept saying it wasn't important to find her body—she said I had to find her in my heart."

It was exactly the message Terri so desperately craved to hear. Her grief was compounded by the rift that had never totally healed between mother and daughter, and now she was faced with the burden of trying to mend that rift with a dead woman. Terri kept notes during these "conversations," writing down what Tammy and others said Loretta was trying to tell her:

Terri, don't make the same mistakes I did
You are the most beautiful spirit I have ever seen
I am so sorry for the way I acted
I need you to forgive me. I can't go on until you do.

Some will say it doesn't take any psychic ability to know what Terri needed to hear—anyone could have said those kind words to help a grieving daughter. In fact, her aunts did. Darla wrote her on Christmas Eve of 2004:

Terri, your mother was very proud of you. We are very proud of you. You have handled this tragedy with such strength and determination that it is amazing. I cannot say enough about how impressed we all are.

Terri says the most comfort came from the messages she was getting directly from her mother, without the help of any outside force.

Every September 21, Loretta would call Terri first thing and sing her "Happy Birthday." "She didn't sing it well, mind you, but who cares? There was always my mother, first thing in the morning, singing me the birthday song over the phone." It wasn't September 21, but December 21—a week after her mother's disappearance—when Terri heard the song. "I was home about nine p.m. and all of a sudden I heard a music box singing 'Happy Birthday to You.' My friend Deanna heard it too. We found the music box in the closet—it's the kind that only plays when you lift the lid. But there were books on top of the box. There's no way it could have played."

It wasn't the last time she was convinced her mother was sending her messages. She remembers about a month after the disappearance when she'd spent yet another day searching the desert. "I pulled into the parking lot at my office and I had my first breakdown," Terri recalls. "I started hitting the steering wheel and screaming, and I just lost it. I reached over to turn off the radio and a country song came on called 'In My Daughter's Eyes.' It's about a mother who died, but you saw her when you looked in her daughter's eyes. It calmed me down and I knew it was my mother. She was saying, 'I'm here.' Then months later, I was at the Elephant restaurant and that song came on again. I took it for another message. If you walk through life and think that things like this just happen, you're going to miss the incredible things around you."

After another empty-handed day searching the desert months later, Terri came home to find her intercom system going berserk—something that hadn't happened before, nor has it since. "I learned to accept these messages," she says.

Like the one she got one day while searching the desert. Her employee, Heather Dolan, recounts this as the most memorable moment on all of the searches. Heather had shopped at the truck stop on the highway before coming out to the desert, buying some snacks to hold her through the morning. "I never eat banana bread, but that morning I bought a package of banana bread," Heather recalls. "We're walking and walking, and I see Terri sit down on the ground, and she says, 'Mom, please just give me a sign.' I sat down next to her and offered her my banana bread. Terri looked at me and said, 'The last time I saw my Mom, she was making banana bread.' "

The last time Terri got a message from beyond was the night her mother's murder was the subject of the national television show *Psychic Detectives*, which bills itself as "the true stories of real cases and the psychics who help investigators solve their most baffling mysteries." It was September 11, 2006, and they called the episode "Desert Rose." Terri was speaking that night, about her mother's death and the problem of elder abuse, to the National Association of Business Women at a four-star hotel in Virginia. "The second the show came on, the pipes in the walls started clanging," Terri says. "I said, 'Mom, are you here?' and they clanged again, and then they were quiet."

Terri remembers smiling, thinking she and her mom were watching together. Terri was in the show, of course, but the spotlight was on Mary Ann Morgan, a medium with international credentials and her own radio program.

As the show demonstrated, with reenactments and interviews, Morgan wasn't just in the neighborhood of what happened to Loretta, she nailed point after point, and made believers out of two hardened homicide detectives. As Detective Pacheco from Tucson told *Psychic Detectives*, "She really impressed me." And Sheriff's Detective Landon Rankin of Pinal County would later acknowledge in an interview for this book that he never believed in psychics until he saw what Morgan did on this case.

Of course, not everyone was a believer, and Psychic Detectives didn't interview the main investigator on the case, Detective Trent Luckow of Tempe. "The psychics became involved, and that played out in the media, but they had no involvement whatsoever, as far as the Tempe Police Department was concerned—we never went to a psychic and asked for help." But Luckow still had to deal with them: "They contacted Terri and she'd call me and say, 'This is what I'm told.' One day it would be one thing and the next would be one hundred-eighty degrees off. I didn't shut her down, because she was looking for answers. It was an outlet for Terri, and that was fine with me. I'd listen to what she said the psychics told her, but in my mind they had no factual basis. I had to keep in mind, the facts are the facts. And I also looked at the prosecutorial basis: information from psychics wouldn't even be brought to court—you'd be laughed out of court."

Terri also got grief from religious groups on the Internet who decried her ungodly reliance on the supernatural. One website noted:

> *The Bible makes it absolutely clear that you CANNOT use psychics.*

Another said:

> *Unfortunately, Terri Bowersock has sought advice and direction from psychics, who have led her on several futile trips into the desert in search of her mother. I can't imagine the turmoil and stress that this situation is causing the Bowersock family. The willing exploitation of a fearful family by psychics, who have no insight at all in this situation, is* deplorable.

But Terri ignored the criticism and continued to listen. And what she heard sometimes made her weep.

It got creepy, how accurate it seemed Mary Ann Morgan was, in seeing not only the murder, but everything after. She wasn't always accurate. She saw Loretta dying Monday morning and Taw going out to the desert to search for a place to hide the body Monday afternoon, while phone records contradict that timeline.

Psychic Detectives took Morgan to the Dillard's in Tucson, and filmed her declaring that Loretta hadn't disappeared there. "Everything is a lie. She was never at this place. This is an absolute lie," Morgan said. But then, the media had been reporting from the start that surveillance cameras showed Loretta had never walked into the store.

Morgan says "lies and deceit" kept screaming at her in her visions of this case. She saw that Taw had been in prison in the past, and was a swindler. She heard Loretta telling her he had lied to her all along. She also saw the end of Taw: "I was in the shower and I saw Taw go off into the sunset—it either meant he was fleeing or committing suicide," she says.

Mary Ann also says she saw Loretta's last journey: "I saw a pick and shovel. I saw him stopping to buy a baseball hat. He's making a cell phone call. And I had to tell Terri, 'I'll never find her. It's not my destiny to find her. And you'll never find her. Hikers will find her. She'll be found in a year.'" Oh yes, she added, one of those hikers will be a Native American.

Every single one of those points would prove accurate.

But more eerie yet was the other thing she saw—something that psychic after psychic saw whenever the gravesite was envisioned: "I see the color blue everywhere around her grave," Morgan said. She saw blue on buildings and abandoned vehicles and towers and even on the hikers' pickup. Then she went a crucial step further: "And I hear children laughing and singing, and hanging off a merry-go-round."

She was correct, right down to the merry-go-round with its peeling blue paint.

CHAPTER 13

Searching the Desert

Everyone but Terri Bowersock knew it was damn near impossible.

Find a body you believe has been buried in a desert that covers thousands of square miles. Even with a few clues on where that little body could be, it's a stab in the dark that you'll ever find the exact spot. It is, quite simply, a staggering assignment handed out in a stunning environment.

The desert is a dry, dusty, prickly place. By its very definition, a desert lacks rain—an area doesn't even qualify for the designation if it has more than 19.7 inches of rain in an entire year. The Sonoran Desert, which covers southern Arizona, southern California and parts of northern Mexico is the hottest of the American deserts, but also has the greatest variety of life. Some 2,000 plant species live in this environment, but unless you have "desert eyes" that can see the nuances of this landscape, things look pretty much alike.

Most would describe this expanse as brown, gray, beige and boring. Even the green that does exist doesn't resemble the green found everywhere else in the country. Desert green is muted, almost gray-green, dusty-green, certainly tired-green. The plants are often low, sometimes bushy, but "scrub" is the word that comes immediately to mind. They don't look nourished under the best of circumstances, and in winter they seem to be positively struggling.

One look at the earth they emerge from tells you why. Forget the black dirt most places call soil. Here, the dirt most resembles crushed gravel. It looks hard and crusty, arid and lifeless. But the few drops of rain that do fall on this land every year support these adapted plants and when you consider how little they live on, their very existence is pretty remarkable.

Into this strange environment, Terri now tromped in hiking boots she'd found in the back of a closet. Psychics had called her the minute they heard about her mother's disappearance, and some of them "saw" the grave. They gave her instructions and maps on where their visions had sent them, and she rushed out in her Porsche.

Tempe detective Trent Luckow was keeping in close contact with Terri and noted these activities. Even in the staid language of police reports, it's easy to hear what he thought of all this:

On 12/21/04 at 1220 hours . . . met with Terri Bowersock off highway 187 on the Gila River Indian Reservation. I observed several vehicles parked on the south side of the road along with officers from the Gila River Indian Police Department and FBI agents. Terri advised they had been searching that particular area based on what a psychic had told her and what the psychic "saw."

Detective Luckow obviously preferred to focus on where the evidence was leading, and with the discovery of the cell phone records, it led elsewhere. He left Terri and her search party that day and drove to the junction of Interstate 8 and Highway 84:

I noted a cell tower positioned on the south side of Interstate 8 at that location. That location is approximately 27 miles west of the Interstate 8 and Interstate 10 junction. The vegetation in that area is desert scrub brush and saguaro cactus. The area is additionally largely unpopulated by humans west of Casa Grande.

If Terri had had her way, all of Arizona's search-and-rescue units would have been fine-tooth-combing the desert, and although they made a valiant effort, she never felt they did enough. So she did it herself, organizing daily searches that went on for weeks, then weekly searches that went on for months. The media were diligent about recording this heartbreaking effort.

Nobody could see her dusty boots on the hard desert soil or watch the dozens of people who walked slowly in a single line—arm-lengths from one another—without feeling a little sick. Every person carried a stick—some were pieces found in the desert, others were walking sticks from home. They used the sticks to poke and sweep under any bush or mound, just in case there was a grave underneath. Nobody said it, but the stick would also come in handy if a rattlesnake showed up in their path.

The television cameras would always pan out, showing the vastness of the land and the smallness of even large search parties. The message was clear: the desert is so big, and one 130-pound woman is so small. But anyone who watched those scenes knew if it were their mother, they'd be out there, too. Another reaction undoubtedly followed: while they prayed in one breath that Terri's mother would be found, they prayed in the next that it wouldn't be Terri who found her.

KTVK–Channel 3 opened one desert report showing a man on his knees, digging with a short-handled hoe and saying, "You'd be looking for individual hairs, fingernails." The reporter's voice-over says: "It's a painstaking search for the body of Loretta Bowersock, and up until now, a fruitless effort." There's Terri, walking with her stick and speculating on when—not if, but when—they find the body: "I'm not going to see her," she vowed. "I've promised my mom, myself and my friends, if we get to that point, I'm going to walk away."

Nobody believed her. They all knew she'd be right there, front and center, if the body showed up. Her long-time friend, Karen Stone, said there was a secret contingency plan. "We had a ten-foot-rule," Karen says. "One of us had to be within ten feet of Terri at all times, because we could only imagine what it would have been like if she'd found her. And we were determined not to let her see her mother's remains."

In another story, Channel 3's Patti Kirkpatrick narrated the video herself—in television code, when the favorite anchor voices the entire story, that means it's extra special. "A discovery in the desert near Casa Grande prompted a new search for a missing Valley woman when a searcher noticed a possible burial site and some clothes and bone," Patti said. The video shifted to Terri: "I'm getting desensitized to look for bones," she says. "At first I was just looking for my mom. Now I'm looking for a smell or pieces of bone or fabric."

Patti's narration continued: "But family and friends of Bowersock say they won't stop until they find her." Terri on camera again: "You know the concept of murder, you think, Oh my God, we've all seen this on TV, but the reality is, this stuff happens to families."

In every story on the searches, Terri always bragged, not about how often she'd come to the desert, but all those who'd joined her. In the beginning, she'd even asked Taw to come out and search. He begged off, but gave her a Maglite black flashlight and told her to use it in her desert hunt. She and her friends sneered at his false "help."

Some friends, like Karen Stone, walked the desert with her ten to fifteen times. "Everybody wanted to do whatever they could to help," Karen says. "It's an amazing situation—you're walking around in the desert and you know why you're there, but there's still fear of what you'll find."

Karen had known Loretta for years, so she wasn't just searching for Terri's mom, but for a "very classy, elegant woman" she'd shared meals and holidays with. "She was kind of old-fashioned, like my mom, and they believed you stuck with your man," Karen says. "I grew up in a family where the father takes care—Taw didn't take care. I never liked Taw. He bugged me. He talked down to people. He had a front, and it really bothered me. I thought he belittled Loretta. But to this day I can't believe Loretta is gone."

Even friends like Karen were amazed at the array of strangers who came forward to help. "Terri grew up on TV in Phoenix and so many types of people came out and just wanted to help; just people who care for mankind."

There were "snowbirds," or winter visitors, from Michigan, and the retired state trooper who showed up out of the blue. There were two guys who arrived in their private helicopter and flew over the search area for hours. There were Indians from the nearby reservation who taught everyone how to systematically search. Customers from her stores came out often, as well as friends from all walks of life, including the gay guys who responded to her call for "search dogs" by bringing their groomed poodle with a handkerchief tied around his neck. (Terri still laughs at that, not laughing at them, but laughing that even though they didn't "get it," they wanted to help.)

There was Jeremiah, who left a breath-catching cardboard note: "I'm willing to look under any avenue or cactus yet unturned. I will march thru hell to help." And there was Randy Anglin, a Department of Public Safety officer who searched during his off-duty time. He developed a computer program that he hoped would help pinpoint the body.

Sometimes only a few people showed up to join Terri in the search. Sometimes, it was sixty or more. "I never went to the desert alone," she says with gratitude. "There were always people there to search with me."

Heather Dolan was one of those people. "There were usually about thirty of us," she remembers. "We'd meet in the morning at one of our stores, or at a pull-off on the freeway, and caravan to the search area. Each time we'd go through the guidelines. If we came upon something, we weren't to touch it, but to wave our arms and yell. The reservation police were adamant that we not dig any holes. We looked for anything that looked disturbed or any dirt that looked mounded."

She remembers they'd usually spend three or four hours on one spot and then move on to a second spot—often another "vision" place from the psychics. They found a small Mexican diner near I-10 where they'd retreat for lunch before launching an afternoon search. The afternoon crew was usually a lot smaller.

"We did find four-wheeler tracks and some clothing under a tree," Heather remembers. "We found a pair of underwear and a shirt. I got my stick and picked up the underwear and called Terri over, but she told me to just put it back. We found a burned mattress and lots of garbage, just an amazing amount of junk. You know, the desert was disgusting. I thought it was funny the reservation police acted like it was a sacred space when it was filled with junk."

But the memory that is front and center when she thinks of the searches is this: "The desert is so vast. It felt like we'd never get to the end. I wasn't scared being out there, but was just hopeful for Terri. When we'd leave empty-handed, it just made it worse—it was an extreme disappointment. We just wanted it to end so Terri could get some closure. It was almost like a movie as the plot thickened, with frustration, sadness and worry."

Meanwhile, professionals were out looking for Loretta, too.

On December 23, Detective Luckow went up in a state police helicopter to search. By that time, Taw was dead and officers had found the second map that showed notations in the area of the cell phone tower. Everyone was quite certain that was where Loretta would be found. Department of Public Safety Air Rescue Pilot Vaughn Perkins flew the helicopter that day with DPS photographer Gary Keltz. Luckow later reported:

The flight concentrated its flight pattern between I-8 and Highway 84, video recording the flight while Keltz completed aerial photographs. I did not observe any signs of an obvious burial site from the flight; however several potential sites were noted.

On January 6, 2005, Luckow got photo blowups of the pictures Keltz had taken on their helicopter tour. DPS coordinator Sharon Nicholson had studied the photos and "determined an area located near a gravel pit," just north of I-8 and east of Highway 84.

Nicholson was able to enlarge the image to a poster size, which she turned over to this investigator. Nicholson could not determine any other potential burial sites to assist the search team.

She gave the Tempe officer a CD that contained a video of the helicopter trip and copies of all the photographs taken that day.

The next day, Luckow met with officers of the Pinal County Sheriff's Search and Rescue office, showing them the enlarged photos of the gravel pit. Luckow reported:

Sgt. Bob Gage, Sgt. Brian Messing and Louis Villa and I then traveled to the gravel pit and conducted a visual search which met with negative results. I learned the search team searched that same gravel pit on 1/08/05 with searchers and dogs. I learned another search was to be completed on 1/09/05 by the Pinal County Search and Rescue Team along Stanfield Rd. south of I-8.

On January 9 at 8:45 a.m., Luckow met with Terri and Deanna at the Terri's Consign & Design store on Ray Street and I-10. "While traveling to the search site, I advised Terri the information obtained by police that led to the area that was being searched." Luckow told her that search and rescue teams had found several bodies in that same area. It was a known route for drug smuggling and illegal immigrants trying to make it to jobs in Phoenix.

Terri stayed out of the way, watching as officers zigzagged on foot through the man-sized shrubs. "I know you guys are doing everything you can," she told them before she left.

In all, officers searched the gravel pit area for three days. Katie Nelson told the sad story on the front page of the *Arizona Republic*'s Valley and State section:

The last lead has evaporated. After three days of intensive searching in the bleak desert south of Phoenix,

*police and volunteers found not a trace of Loretta Bow-
ersock.*

*Despite the cell phone–tower records, the gas-purchase
receipts and a map left open to the area, 15 trained
searchers and six cadaver dogs couldn't find the body of
the 69-year-old Tempe woman who vanished December
14. Three days of organized searching by police, the Pinal
County Sheriff's Department and trained volunteers has
turned up nothing.*

*Beginning at 7:30 a.m., they started scouring the land
using a grid formation. [Louie] Villa and his dog, Cholla,
were assigned to scout the riverbed. The female German
shepherd eagerly wound her way in and out of brush,
sniffing for human scent.*

*The downward slope would have been impossible to
navigate with the red minivan owned by Taw Benderly,
Tempe police's only suspect, but he could have parked on
a dirt road nearby, Villa calculated.*

*Benderly's age, strength, vehicle and whereabouts are
playing a significant role in the search. Police don't believe that Benderly, at 67 years old, could have dragged
Bowersock far. But the gritty sand would have been easy
to maneuver with a shovel and pick that police later found
in his car. . . .*

*Unless fresh leads surface, the efforts by police to find
Bowersock's body won't continue, investigators said.*

Terri had known this day was coming. She knew
officers wouldn't continue forever to walk the desert
when even the clues Taw left behind didn't turn up
anything. But that didn't stop her and her friends
from continuing their search.

The last story about her desert vigil ran in the *Republic* on April 2, 2005, but it was no longer on the front page, it now was a small story printed inside the Valley section:

> *Loretta Bowersock's family continued their search of Arizona deserts for her body Friday with the help of a psychic. They scoured the ground for "something red in the dirt," a sign the psychic said to look for. . . . Friday's search party was small: two of Loretta Bowersock's sisters and her daughter accompanied by a psychic. Beginning about 11 a.m., the women walked south of the Valley along Interstate 8, near Stanfield Road. It's an area police have identified as a likely burial site using Benderly's cell phone records.*
>
> *The group drove around looking for a place that a person could be buried in creek beds and under brush. They also posted fliers aimed at hikers and passers-by, offering a $1,000 reward. Anyone with information is asked to call Tempe police. . . .*

Then even Terri had to give up. Finally, she had to admit the desert was too enormous and Loretta was too small, and the chances of ever finding her were too remote.

"Maybe someday somebody will be building a house out in the desert and they'll dig up her body," she said. But she knew this wasn't an area where anybody was going to build any houses for a very long time. Probably not in her lifetime.

She had to resign herself that there would never be the "closure" needed when a loved one dies.

She'd never have a chance to take the ashes to Hawaii so she and Scott could scatter them at the ocean.

She'd forever wonder what happened to her beautiful mother, and if her dreadful coyote vision had been accurate.

CHAPTER 14

Finding the Body

The minute they drove into the ravine that Tuesday,
Linda and Randy Johnson got a familiar "sick feeling" in their stomachs.

"We looked at each other and I said, 'Randy,
something's strange.' The hair on my arms stood up.
Randy had hair everywhere standing up."

The feeling had only hit them one other time, one
night when they were lost on the Gila River Indian
Community near Sacaton: "We came to this bridge
and I didn't want to cross over," Linda remembers.
"We sat there about five minutes in the dark, feeling
like we wanted to throw up, but we had to go across.
Randy held my hand and I drove across that bridge as
fast as I could. We later learned that's where big Indian battles had taken place in the 1800s. It was a
place of death. And here we were in this ravine and
we had that same feeling again. I said, 'Randy, we'll
find something fabulous or something really bad.' He
said, 'Don't think like that'—he's a positive thinker."

The 50-something couple had come to the Table
Top Wilderness—a gravel pit abandoned twenty
years ago that sits just south of I-8 and just east of
Highway 84. They'd come to rock-hunt with their
19-year-old son, Carl, who was visiting from Florida.

Their apprehension was creeping him out. "You guys are scarin' me," he told them, hoping they'd drive on and find another place to look for rocks that could be cleaned up, polished and bring a decent price at the flea market.

But Linda had been drawn to this place for months, ever since they'd moved to the nearby town of Maricopa—a wide spot in the road, now flourishing from the nearby casino, but with a rich history: this was the original stop for southern rail service in the late 1800s when the railroad finally came to Arizona Territory. And now that Phoenix had screwed up again and become the only major American city without passenger rail service, Maricopa was once more the only southern rail link between Los Angeles and points south.

The couple had returned to Arizona—back together after a short divorce—in July of 2005 and moved to five acres in Maricopa that October. "I kept telling Randy that someday we have to go to these mountains I'm attracted to." Although Linda believes both she and Randy have psychic abilities, that wasn't what drew her to the mountains that stand so stark and stately—one resembles a man's face; he's lying on his back with his big nose reaching to the sky.

"When there's a group of mountains, there's usually lots of washes, and that's where you find the best rocks," she instructs. "You can find something real special. And now here we were, and I hoped we'd find amethyst or turquoise, maybe an Indian burial ground."

They'd had to guess how to get here, since there

are no roads in the open, prickly desert. You make your own road when you explore places like this, if you can get to them. "We found a break in the fence—you have to be careful not to trespass or go on Indian land, because you can get in trouble," Linda notes. But she thought they were fine now, as she found the break behind a long abandoned motel, its blue paint was a faint reminder that it once had serviced truck drivers and families traveling from San Diego to Phoenix. She drove their pickup up, down and through the ruts and washes that slashed the land. It was a bumpy and uncomfortable ride, but experienced rock hunters knew this is what you had to expect if you were going to find the best stones.

Linda parked her blue truck and they sat there a moment, feeling that horrible queasiness in their stomachs. But Randy's encouraging words and Linda's certainty of something great moved them on. Randy went up on a ridge while Linda and Carl started down the bone-dry wash. That's how most washes in Arizona are most of the time, dry and deceitful, seemingly just a wide rut in the earth. But let some rain fall and they can become a raging stream within minutes.

For a few minutes, things looked very promising: "I was picking up some interesting pieces," Linda remembers, congratulating herself that her instincts had been right about this place being a treasure trove.

And then it all changed: "Carl comes over with his mouth open and his eyes so wide," she remembers, "I thought maybe he'd seen a snake or something. But when I asked him what, he just yelled, 'We gotta get outta here! I got to go get Dad.'

"I asked him, 'What's the matter?' but he just told me to step away—not to go backward or forward, just stay there while he got Dad. I turned around and looked at a wall of earth, but I didn't see nothing. I squatted down to look at a rock, and all of a sudden I saw a skull sticking out of the ground. Oh my God. I fell backwards and started yelling for Randy."

Poking out of the ground were the remains of a human face emerging from what looked like shredded black plastic. If you looked closely, you could see the rock shroud that covered the body. There wasn't any skin left on the face, and the sun had started bleaching the bones. A small tuft of blondish hair was still attached to the head.

Linda remembers she was startled, but she didn't panic. "I can't believe how calm I was. Randy was, too. I can't say that about Carl—he worried whoever buried this was watching us and would come after us. I said, 'You can tell this has been here awhile.'" Even acknowledging this body was greatly decomposed, Carl couldn't give up on the fear that the killer was there, would take down their license plate number, would track them to their home and kill them all in the night.

Randy hunkered down to get a better look, using his pen knife to push away a piece of plastic. From what he saw, he declared this was probably a white woman. His first clue was the once-soft hair still attached to the skull—hair that wouldn't be found on a black or Mexican or Indian. And then there were the perfect teeth. Randy said, "It's gotta be a woman, because the teeth were taken care of so well. I think it's an older woman by the length of the teeth. It's not a transient or a drug user—they'd never have teeth like that."

The Johnsons had no idea who this could be. They'd never heard of Loretta Bowersock—in fact, were among the few in the state who didn't recognize her daughter's name. They'd been in Florida when Loretta "disappeared," and by the time they returned to Arizona, the media frenzy was over. But they didn't need to know any of that to know somebody must be looking for this perfect-teeth woman who once was a sandy blonde. This had to be somebody's mother.

"I got out the cell phone and told Randy to call the police, but we didn't know what county we were in, Pinal or Maricopa, so Randy called our good friend, John, to see what to do. Randy told him, 'You ain't gonna believe this, we found a body!' "

As it turns out, John had found bodies in the desert before—not such an unusual thing, considering the desert is a great dumping ground for criminals, and also a killing ground for desperate Mexicans trying to sneak into the United States. John was quick to share his experiences with this kind of find—one time he got threats because he'd found a body that wasn't meant to be found; another time, he became a suspect because he was the one finding the body. He came through both unscathed, but he was cautious now about how they should proceed. At some point, somebody wondered out loud if they should just drive on and forget the skull.

And some would have. Some would have decided a dead white woman buried in the desert was a whole world of trouble, and nothing good could come from getting involved. Some would have worried that they were risking their own safety by exposing themselves to police who might just look at their backgrounds and find something they shouldn't; or, as Carl continued to insist, they could be ticking off the kind of people who don't hesitate to kill and dump bodies in the desert.

But that's not the kind of people who'd found Loretta Bowersock. She was lucky to be stumbled upon, after all this time, by compassionate and decent people like Linda and Randy Johnson.

"We never thought about walking away," Linda says proudly.

"If this was somebody in our family," she told her anxious son, "you'd want people to report it so you can have closure." But still, she admits now, "We hoped the closure we were giving to someone wasn't opening a can of worms for us."

Randy told John to make the call to police. John suggested the couple go back to the main road and wait for officers. Linda and Carl followed that suggestion, waiting in their pickup outside the abandoned motel along I-8 that had once had ten rooms and an office, and still has a plastic railroad porter standing out front. The Arizona sun has done its best to eat off all the paint on this lonely spot, but still, you can tell someone once got a deal at Sears on blue paint, because they'd covered everything with it—signs, a slide, a merry-go-round, teeter-totters, a picnic bench, even the jacket and cap on the plastic porter.

Randy wouldn't go with them. He insisted on staying with the body. He told his wife, "This woman has been out here alone a long time, and she shouldn't be alone anymore."

For the first time in thirteen months, someone stood vigil over Loretta's grave. It was a 5-foot-7-inch, blue-eyed, rock-hunting guy in jeans who had no idea who she was, no idea that Arizona had been consumed with her disappearance, no idea that her famous daughter had walked the desert not far from here time and again, no idea that search-and-rescue units and cadaver dogs had been so very, very close to this exact spot so many times. All this kind, part-Cherokee man knew is that a body that once held a soul shouldn't be discarded and abandoned anymore.

John placed the 911 call at 3:58 p.m. on January 10, 2006. Within eleven minutes, Pinal County Sheriff's officers were on their way.

Detective Landon Rankin jumped into his squad car and rushed to the scene. He was hopeful but cautious, because he never believed they'd ever find Loretta in the humungous desert. "Look at the desert," the second-generation Arizonan instructs, "and then you know why you can't find anything. It's a needle looking for a needle in a stack of needles. We used the cadaver dogs and couldn't find anything. Search and Rescue spent days out there and turned up nothing."

On his way out to the grave—almost exactly where searchers had focused—Rankin wondered if this might not just be another Mexican national who didn't make it to a low-paying job in Phoenix. After all, the call pinpointed a "smuggling corridor" well-known to law enforcement, and said a body was found wrapped in plastic. "I knew lots of Mexican Nationals carry a four- or five-foot piece of plastic to keep the storms off," Rankin says.

He met Linda at the motel and remembers that something clicked when he saw all the blue— somewhere in his notes, the color blue meant something. She led him back to the ravine. The minute he saw the skull, he realized this was a promising find.

"I could tell it was a female by the jawbone, and I knew it wasn't an Afro-American because of the small bone at the front of the nose that African-Americans don't have. The teeth were healthy and in good repair. I could see fillings, and porcelain caps, and I said, 'This isn't someone poor.' I thought, This is probably Loretta Bowersock."

By now, this 1952 graduate of Gila Bend High School had more than a passing interest in the case. He'd met with Terri and liked the "strong woman" he found. He also sympathized with a child needing to bury a parent. He worried that she was carrying too much guilt on her shoulders. "She'd tell me, 'If I'd only called her and gone over,' and I told her she couldn't blame herself," he remembers. From his own investigation and reports from both Tempe and Tucson, he already knew her mother had died in a "crime of passion." As he explains, "Self-preservation is our first instinct, and when Loretta heard the news about the foreclosure on her house, for him it was self-preservation to get rid of small, frail Loretta."

To this day, Rankin wishes Taw Benderly had stuck around so he could have been prosecuted. "He was scared and he took the chickenshit way out by hanging himself," Rankin says. "I wish he'd given closure with a note—'Here she is, I'm sorry'—but I think his pride wouldn't let him, and that was a last dig at Terri, like, 'Try to sell this house now, with a public record showing there was a suicide here.' As a homicide detective, I like closure, too, and that's a prosecution that nails him. When you take a case all the way through, you can go to bed saying, 'Today I earned my pay.'"

Already Rankin knew it wasn't good police work, but good ole Mother Nature, that had solved this case. The desert is a deceptive environment, looking like only the most irascible and thorny things can live here. But give it rain—as precious as gold in these parts—and the desert is a riot of color and growth and activity. Plants literally burst from the earth when rain finally feeds their roots; animals emerge from their ground or cactus homes, birds swoop the sky, the desert shows off its patina of purples and yellows. In the normal cycle of the desert, the brown chapter dominates with thrilling interludes of the colorful time. But Arizona was already deep into a drought by the time Loretta was buried in the desert—a drought that continues to this day, and threatens the future of this desert state, where experts say global warming means "nothing but bad news."

So it's amazing that rain eventually gave Loretta back to her family. Despite the drought, Arizona in 2005–2006 had a lot of welcome rain. "We'd had a real wet winter," Detective Rankin notes. "Roosevelt Lake was at its highest point ever, and rivers and washes were running." In one of those washes, buried in the softened sand, lay the body that everyone had so longed for.

The water had rushed down this particular ravine
and washed away all that sand and shifted the blanket of rocks over the body. "Rodents had started eat-
ing away at the plastic and around her face," Rankin
adds. "Nature started to work and the sun bleached
the skull. The part of her still in the plastic was almost mummified."

As officers milled around, careful to leave the
crime scene intact, and waiting for the medical examiner, they all came to the same conclusion: "We
were ninety-nine percent sure it was Loretta,"
Rankin says. "We knew we were in the right area because one of Taw's mistakes was to use his cell
phone while he was burying her. We knew which
tower had routed the call." When he looked up,
Rankin could see that tower some 500 yards away.

There was another thing you could see if you
stepped back a second and turned your eyes to the
bluffs around the body. There stood several stately
saguaro cactus—the sentinels of the desert, which
are unique to this location. These succulents can
weigh as much as a car and stand fifty feet tall, with
"arms" that often extend in contorted directions.
They say it takes a hundred years to grow a saguaro
arm, but that's an exaggeration, although growth on
these bad boys is a slow thing. So a cactus with a lot
of arms, or long arms, has seen this patch of desert
for many, many years—certainly more than Loretta
Bowersock ever lived.

One of those saguaros looked as though it were
reaching out to cradle Loretta in its gently sweeping
embrace. Even Rankin, a twelve-year veteran of de-

tective work, with a couple dozen murder cases under his belt, had to admire the gesture. He remembers thinking that at least something had been looking over her all these months.

Rankin's cell phone rang and it was Pinal County Sheriff Chris Vasquez, who was refereeing a basketball game at a local high school. "I heard you found a body," the sheriff said hopefully. "Is there any chance this is Bowersock?" Rankin remembers telling him, "It's ninety-nine percent," and the sheriff declared, "No holds barred—whatever you need." But Rankin already knew that's just what the sheriff would order.

Meanwhile, Tempe police showed up—after all, this case was partly in their jurisdiction, too. Rankin asked them for Loretta's dental records, and remembers he later went down to Tempe and hand-carried them to the autopsy.

In an exclusive interview with Katie Nelson of the *Arizona Republic*, Rankin laid out the slow, laborious process of removing the body:

At 10 a.m. Wednesday, the slow scooping, sifting and shoveling began to unearth the grave. Six deputies were there. Layer by layer, they removed the sand and rocks using gardening trowels, paintbrushes, buckets, even a soup spoon. Each batch of sand was put through a screen to make sure nothing, such as a tooth or an earring, was missed. "It's similar to an archeological dig," Rankin said. "Very tedious and time-consuming."

As the investigators inched farther down, it became clear they were getting a big break. Whoever buried the body had wrapped it in a layer of black landscaping tarp, taped it up, and wrapped it again. Unwrapped remains tend to get scattered by weather, water and animals, said Rankin, who deals with dozens of dumped bodies each year.

The body was taken to the Pima County Office of the Medical Examiner for an autopsy, including x-rays that showed no bullet wounds, no fractured bones. It also revealed how she had died. And the dental records confirmed this was Loretta.

Once the identity was firm, Rankin called Terri. "We have found your mother," he told her. The *Republic* quoted Darla Neal on the find: "It forces you to deal with the grief all over again. But at least you don't have that awful feeling she is somewhere out there and you can't protect her."

The Johnsons realized just who they had found a couple days later, as they watched the live news conference that told Arizona the body had finally been found. They soon met a grateful Terri, who was so very thankful they'd cared enough to call in the find, and touched that Randy would stay by her mother's grave so the poor woman no longer had to be alone. Terri gave them the $1,000 reward she'd offered. Linda remembers thinking she would have done just what Terri had done if it had been her mom: "People hunt and hunt and don't give up—I wouldn't either."

But as time went on, the Johnsons soured over their experience. "All the media was writing about us but nobody ever contacted us," Linda says. "They said we were hikers, but we weren't, we're rock hunters." It was like insult on injury—they were ignored and misidentified at the same time. One of their friends told her he thought a $10,000 reward had been offered, and the thousand dollars that had seemed so grand didn't anymore. Linda was quick to note that they hadn't done this for the money, and later learned that there never had been a $10,000 offer.

"We weren't looking for a reward. We were just happy to help someone find their loved one. But it seems a lot of the time, people are so appreciative and then . . ." The worst insult was being left out of the TV show. "They told us *Psychic Detectives* was going to do a story on the case and we'd be in it, but they used actors instead," Linda says. "We were incensed."

It's doubtful they would have been happy even if they had been included. The show's focus was on psychic Mary Ann Morgan, and the actual finding of the body was reduced to a couple of seconds. All that *Psychic Detectives* gave to the discovery was three people backing away from the camera, as though they were repelled by the body. They are only identified as "hikers," and not by name. Ignored and misidentified, yet again.

Linda still wishes someone would acknowledge the pain this experience caused her family. "People don't know how traumatic it is when you come upon a skull. It's awful," she says.

The couple have moved to Payson, where Randy is a certified nurse's assistant and Linda does housekeeping. Their son has gone back to Florida. "Carl

said he felt better when he learned Taw hanged himself so he wouldn't come after us," Linda says.

For herself, she still thinks of Loretta: "It's such a
shame, all that happening to her."

CHAPTER 15

We Have Found Your Mother

Her body shuddered as she flinched, and it was impossible to miss it. There it was, right on the television screen, live.

It was such an unusual look for Terri Bowersock. Most of Arizona was used to seeing her on television, but only with a full, beaming smile; only with a perky personality that was always bubbly and upbeat. No one had ever seen her like this. It was painful to watch her involuntary shudder of revulsion as she stood there on live TV and learned how her mother had been murdered.

It was January 12, 2006, and Arizona was learning that Terri's pretty mother had been found.

Television news shows interrupted their regular 6 p.m. broadcasts to carry the live press conference, so everyone saw it. They saw Terri, dressed in a floral shirt and standing next to an American flag, flinch when she heard the news—Taw had taken a plastic bag that had once brought home tomatoes or onions from the local grocery store and wrapped it around Loretta's head, holding it tight around her throat until she stopped struggling and finally, finally, stopped breathing. Pieces of plastic were still around Loretta's head when she was found.

It had been thirteen long months of searching the desert to find the body, and there'd been so many false starts, so many disappointments, that at first, Terri couldn't believe this was really true. When Pinal County officials called to report that rock hunters had found a buried body and they thought it could be Loretta, Terri calmly stored the information in a part of her brain that no longer had any connection to her heart. She'd learned to do this over the long months as one dashed hope after another became a way of life. There had been so many psychics who'd pinpointed the grave, and they'd all been wrong. There'd been the guy who got her out of a business meeting because he'd found something in the desert, but it wasn't Loretta. There'd been the miles on miles she'd walked with her hiking boots and wooden stick, and they'd found nothing but junk. Terri would go home after each of these encounters and cry herself to sleep, falling deeper and deeper into a depression that said never, ever, would this nightmare end.

That morning's *Arizona Republic* had carried the first news that "Discovery Could End Yearlong Mystery." Katie Nelson reported that the body was scheduled for an autopsy that day and a final determination was expected by that night. It quoted Terri as saying, "I keep praying it's her—it would answer a lot of things. But if anything, I'd like to be able to bury her properly." The story also noted that Terri had been burning a prayer candle since she'd gotten the call from police the day before.

The tests completed late that afternoon proved the body in the grave was Loretta Bowersock. Detective

Rankin called Terri. Officers were calling a news conference for 5 p.m. at the Pinal County Sheriff's Office in Florence, but they'd brief Terri first. She should come as soon as she could.

Television stations from both Phoenix and Tucson jumped when they were alerted to the news. Satellite trucks set out for Florence, a small town, halfway between the big cities, that normally doesn't get media coverage for anything but tragedy. No, the media doesn't usually come to Florence for good news stories.

The major exception was when Hollywood came to town in 1985 to film *Murphy's Romance* with Sally Field and James Garner. That was really something, as Hollywood spruced up the antique downtown for the story of a divorced mother who moves to a small Arizona town with her 12-year-old boy and falls for an older, laid-back, widowed pharmacist who's a town fixture. Garner got his first Oscar nomination for his role as Murphy, who "falls in love for the last time in my life" with Sally.

Florence might have been the quintessential romantic town because it's an old Arizona farming community with fabulous examples of territorial architecture and one of the state's prettiest courthouses. But its fate was sealed in 1908 when the Territorial Prison was moved here from Yuma. The hoosegow's been expanded dozens of times since and now sprawls across 2,365 acres. This is where Arizona houses the most hardened of prisoners. This is the home of Death Row. In Territorial Days, Arizona hung them high, then later, changed over to the electric chair, and lately has extracted the ultimate penalty by lethal injection. Most people driving to Florence come for a limited visit with an inmate at the prison, although recently, some have come to shop. On the free side of the prison fence is a retail store, selling the wares prisoners make: finely tooled leather goods; intricate scrimshaw that dealers from Scottsdale scarf up; painstaking folded paper items, and purses out of old license plates that have become a chic fashion accessory in Arizona.

But the media usually comes only when there's a prison riot or a breakout, and the last time most of these reporters were in town was that awful July day in 1997 when Becky Thornton tried to break her death-row husband, Floyd, out of the prison watermelon field. It had been a stupid plan—she stood at the ten-foot-fence topped with barbed wire, shooting her AK-47 at guards watching the men pick fruit, while Floyd ran toward her, screaming "Shoot me, baby, shoot me!" She did, a second before officers gunned her down. The "get-away car" had hardly any gas and she had no money, and how they thought they'd ever get away with it nobody has ever figured out. Finding Loretta was good news and the media came.

Terri Bowersock had never been to Florence before, and her dyslexia doesn't make directions easy in the first place, so it wasn't surprising she got lost on her way to the news conference. By the time she'd finally found the sheriff's office, the media had been cooling its heels for a long time and everyone was getting impatient to break into programming. "The deputies offered to brief me privately, but I told them to go ahead with the news conference because everyone was waiting and I knew the reporters were anxious," she remembers.

So she heard the news with the rest of Arizona and had no time to gird herself to the awful truth.

All this time, Terri had believed the psychics' version of how her mother died. She believed Loretta had been hit over the head in her own home and died instantly, never knowing what happened or feeling any pain. It was the one comforting thought Terri had in all these months: At least Mom didn't suffer.

Now, she was hearing instead that Loretta had been suffocated. "That really got me," Terri says. Newspaper reports commented on her "pale face" as she heard the news. And back in newsrooms at television stations, people felt a stab of sympathy in watching her pain.

To the television cameras Terri said: "She was an absolutely beautiful lady and I'm glad she was found. The love that I have gotten from all of us in Arizona, from all the reporters and all the letters, is unbelievable. I thank you and my mother thanks you. Tremendously." She held both hands over her heart as she gave that speech and the emotion in her voice was loud and clear.

Inside the Florence station house, she looked for reassurance from the officers. "Suffocation—that's quick, right?" she almost pleaded.

Somebody should teach law enforcement that there is a time to be merciful and lie. One of those times is when a daughter is clinging to the myth that her beloved mother didn't suffer in her final moments. But nobody had taught that to the Florence

officers. So they didn't lie. They didn't even soften it
much. They told her the truth.

It takes an eternity to enter eternity when you're
being smothered. Four, five minutes maybe. All the
time without air; all the time knowing you're dying;
all the time looking at your murderer. It's an agoniz-
ing death. It's a torment Terri will live with the rest
of her life.

She had to sit down once she got inside, and somebody brought her a glass of water. She wanted details,
but she didn't. She wanted to know everything, but
she didn't. She'd never really thought how it would be
at this minute, when everything would be revealed,
but she was quickly finding that it had been easier not
knowing—especially not knowing her mother had
been so tortured. She didn't stay long, but thanked the
officers and rushed back to her car. All she wanted
was to be alone.

If she'd had her way, Terri would have gone
straight to the gravesite where her mother had been
found, but dark had already fallen. She went home to
her lavish house in the Ahwatukee section of
Phoenix—a portion of Arizona's capital city that lies
behind South Mountain. It is one of the "planned
communities" that have swallowed so many acres of
desert. It's big enough and complete enough—every
store you'd ever need, its own libraries, police and
fire stations, schools, parks—that in other parts of the
country it would be considered its own town.

The next day, Terri went to the grave with her
friend, Karen Stone. She caught her breath when she
realized it was exactly as she'd seen in her coyote

nightmare. There was the sand dune to the right; there was the dune at the foot of the grave; there was the cactus. In the dream, she'd been positioned exactly as her mother was buried. "I described it to a *T*," Terri told Karen.

The place looked so familiar, so friendly, actually, that there were no tears. Maybe after thirteen months of crying and cursing, there weren't any tears left. But this wasn't the hostile, hasty grave Terri had always expected to find. And she was eternally grateful that the last part of her dream hadn't been true.

Terri had been resigned to the strong suggestion from police that her mother's body was in a shallow grave, exposed enough for the wildlife that make the desert home. She'd long believed her mother had been eaten by coyotes and the bones scattered, just as she'd dreamed. So it was comforting—yes, that was the word she wanted, *comforting*—to learn that Loretta had been so carefully wrapped in landscaping tarp and buried under a mound of rocks.

"There was some love in how she was buried," she says generously about her mother's killer.

She wondered if Taw had said a prayer as he placed the rocks; if he'd cried over what he'd done to wonderful Loretta. Terri isn't a particularly religious person, but this visit to the grave was like a benediction for her. It finally filled that gnawing spot in her heart that had been an open wound all these months—the one she'd tried to close by her constant searches.

Her aunts still can't muster up that much sympathy for the man who took their sister. "Terri is on the phone telling me how lovingly he buried her," remembers Aunt Shirley Gates, "and I'm telling her, 'There's no loving way to murder somebody.' " Shirley will never forgive him, will never have a kind thought for him, although she says she understands her niece is trying to "let go."

Now, as Terri stood at the grave for the first time and thought back on it, she realized she hadn't been alone during this entire ordeal, but had been surrounded by love the whole time. "I never went out to the desert alone," she recalls in wonderment and gratitude. "When they found the body, I asked, 'What two miles of the desert did I miss?' " Virtually everyone she knew and dozens she'd never met before had come forward to help her. Her friend, Deanna Jordon, had been the main contact person after Loretta's disappearance, and had logged 7,500 minutes on her cell phone in just the first two weeks.

Other friends had helped with the snail mail and emails that flooded into Terri's home and office—all the time her mother was missing, not a day went by without condolences. After her mother was found, the flood of notes started all over again.

"I know you are strong and the universe is holding you up right now. Always remember you have angels and friends," wrote Kathleen early on. "My family and I personally ask our Creator to give you strength to comfort. Don't lose hope," wrote Juan. "Your mother would be proud of how you have conducted yourself during this sad part of your life," Diane emailed the day after Loretta was positively identified. "You and your family are in our prayers all the way here in Arkansas. Your mother was a beautiful person and that will continue in you," Tammy emailed. There were messages from Alaska, Colorado, California, Kansas, Minnesota, Missouri, Nevada, New Mexico, New York, Pennsylvania, Virginia and some two dozen Arizona cities.

Terri had read them all and took what comfort she could from them. But it wasn't until Loretta had actually been found that she had any solace.

All this time, Terri had been searching just eight miles too far east. She will forever be convinced that if she'd just driven those extra miles, she'd have realized where the body had to be. Because she'd have seen all the blue the psychics kept seeing around the gravesite.

The clue never meant anything to Terri, because there never was anything blue in the search area. Blue isn't even a color of the desert. Most people new to this environment have trouble seeing any color, but once your eyes get acclimated to the desert's palette, you discover that it embraces purple and yellow like they were school colors. Throw in hefty doses of magenta, some orange, lots of white. Just don't look for blue.

As Terri stood at the gravesite, she realized she was surrounded by a riot of blue clues, from the color of the abandoned motel to the water tower and the children's playground equipment. "If I'd ever seen this . . ." she says, letting the thought wander.

Her skeptical brother, who makes it clear he doesn't buy this psychic stuff, scoffs at the blue clue that Terri has so spotlighted. "I did some research, and psychics always pick out a primary color," he says, in dismissing the notion they'd "seen" anything of value about his mother's death and burial.

Terri is convinced Taw scoped out this spot long before he arrived with a body to bury. "If you pulled into the motel, you had to drive around the back," she notes. "There's an old road, and once you're out there, it's so secluded no one could see you. It's a miracle she was found. I always thought eventually somebody would be building and find her body, but nobody was ever going to build out there."

The only thing out here is a grizzly but friendly guy, who lives in a small camper behind the motel with nothing but "my woman and my dogs," as he tells visitors. He wears a "Do Your Thing" t-shirt, and it seems appropriate for someone who admits he "doesn't like being around too many people." He warns that anyone trying to drive the road up to the gravesite now is probably going to break an axle, and he personally wouldn't do it. Besides, he adds, it's a sad place.

Terri's visit to this site was sad, but she was grateful, too. She sat on a rock for a while, next to the spot of dirt that still held the indent of her mother's body. And she finally found some peace. But her friend Karen has heard her speak about her mother's murder, and she notices how Terri's voice changes as she tells the story. "It's one thing to lose your mother to old age, but to have her taken from you is another," Karen says. "This is a hurt that never ends. It's broken her heart."

To this day, Terri finds any comfort she can. "It's a little bit comforting that he didn't just toss her out,"

she says softly. "There was love and hate in that relationship. He buried her to save her and protect her."

It sounds just like something Loretta would have
said. In the old days.

CHAPTER 16

A New Start

Darla Neal knows what happened to her beloved sister: "They say if you put a frog in boiling water, it will jump out, but if you put a frog in tepid water and then slowly raise the temperature, it will boil to death. That's what happens to abused women: they slowly boil to death."

Of the millions of words written about domestic violence and spousal abuse—entire shelves of libraries and bookstores are devoted to this painful subject—perhaps this example sums it up best.

It doesn't bring much comfort—Shirley Gates hates to even think her sister would be considered an abuse victim, because "she wasn't a weak, helpless woman," as though that were the criterion for violence in the home. But it does help explain what happened to a woman who didn't fit any of our stereotypes of abused women: Loretta was beautiful and fashionable and impeccably groomed and wore her jewels like trophies, which in fact they were; she had a loving family and usually made friends for a lifetime. She had a college degree and a couple of businesses under her belt, and she was a whiz at seeing value in what most see as junk. She made chicken soup for her sick daughter and filled a home with Christmas love, and she had that beautiful, enchanting smile.

No, Loretta wasn't the "type" we think of when we talk about women being beaten up and tortured at home. We normally think of a disheveled young wife with a black eye and purple bruises, with small, scared children hanging on to her legs. But that's hardly the whole story. Chances are most people have never, ever thought of lovely senior citizens fitting into the abuse scene.

And yet, senior citizens are the fastest growing category of domestic abuse victims these days, according to police and community activists. And Loretta was one of them—one who paid the ultimate price when her long-time boyfriend murdered her. The year she died, more than 4,900 cases of suspected elder abuse were reported in her home county in Arizona, notes Mary Lynn Kasunic, president of the Area Agency on Aging. "The victims represent all ethnic, religious, educational, occupational and socio-economic groups," she adds. "Sadly, only one in ten cases is actually reported, yet according to national estimates, at least one in twenty older adults is a victim." Loretta was one of those cases not reported—until she was dead.

Kasunic says that until the media attention on Loretta's death, most people in Arizona didn't even know elder abuse was an issue. "While there has been a lot of media attention about domestic violence in younger couples, the occurrence of late life domestic violence is often unrecognized," she says. "Older women are among the many victims of spousal abuse, often staying in an abusive marriage for thirty to forty or even fifty years. When they were young brides, no one talked openly about domestic violence. They believed that they had to endure the abuse because of the lifelong commitment to their marriage vows."

Besides, Arizona didn't even have "shelters" for abused women until the 1970s—safe houses that are meant to give abused women a place to flee, but as every state in the union will attest, there are never enough beds for all the scared women who need them. The year Loretta died, Arizona sheltered 9,483 women who fled their abusive homes, but another 11,056 women were turned away because there was no room. That same year, Governor Janet Napolitano launched the 2004 State Plan on Domestic and Sexual Violence that sought to strengthen the laws and greatly expand the number of beds to make them available in all of Arizona's fifteen counties. The next year, Arizona attorney general Terry Goddard, working with the Arizona Coalition Against Domestic Violence, brought the national CUT IT OUT program to Arizona. "This commonsense program draws on the cosmetology community's unique access to women by training salon professionals to recognize signs of domestic violence in their clients and assist victims in getting help," Goddard explained.

Domestic violence has become so epidemic, national reports show it is the number one cause of emergency room visits by women, of all ages, and is the cause of more injuries to women than car accidents, muggings and rape *combined*.

Loretta had the same misconceptions of most, and wouldn't have considered herself an abused woman.

"I knew Mother wasn't happy with Taw the last few years, but she felt it wasn't so bad, and she didn't want to be alone," Terri says. "She'd say, 'He doesn't drink, he doesn't run around, he doesn't hit me.' So she didn't think he was abusing her, but he was. Abuse is more than hitting. Abuse is stealing your identity. Abuse is taking your money. Abuse is turning you away from your daughter."

In fact, all those factors are the very definition of abuse.

Suzanna Goldman is the president of the Arizona chapter of NAELA (National Academy of Elder Law Attorneys) and she's watched Loretta's case closely. "Loretta is so typical," she says. Elder abuse comes in many forms: the physical abuse that is common to all domestic violence, but also the financial abuse that is more focused on older women who have resources. There's also emotional, sexual and psychological abuse, as well as neglect.

Goldman categorizes exploiters in two categories: hunters or gatherers. "Hunters decide on a single victim and zero in; gatherers run lotteries or hold seminars at hotels and get a lot of people in. Loretta was the victim of a hunter. He took advantage of an opportunity."

And then he followed the usual script: Taw isolated her, causing rifts with her friends and daughter. He took control of their lives, handling all the mail, monitoring all the phone calls, always being around, so that friends complained they were "joined at the hip." He promised his love and companionship to ward off her loneliness. And then he verbally browbeat her year after year, telling her she was dumb, suggesting that her mind was going, undercutting her decisions and demanding domination over their activities.

And Loretta followed a script, too. She bowed to his will, she abandoned her daughter, she became such a puppet that one of her friends walked away in disgust. Loretta wrote out her frustrations in journals and yelled at Taw, but put up with him, year after year. Even when she knew he was conning her, she used a line that is a classic in elder abuse cases: "I made my bed and have to lie in it." She didn't try to throw him out until the very end, and that's when he killed her. Domestic violence experts all agree the most dangerous time for a woman is when she's either leaving him or throwing him out—that's when the control is broken and that's when an abuser reacts with "You bitch, you're not doing this to *me*!"

"Loretta could have called Terri, she could have called the police, she could have called Adult Protective Services, but to make any of those calls, she'd have admitted how stupid she was—and who's going to do that?" Goldman asks. "So she didn't call Terri or her best friend when she found out he'd been stealing the mortgage payments, but tried to handle it herself by confronting him. That tells me she was embarrassed—and that's why cases of financial abuse are so hard to prosecute. Is she really going to sit on the stand and admit how stupid she was? God, that must have been a terrible feeling."

The pattern Goldman sees in abused older women includes loneliness, isolation and a dependent personality—all of which are part of Loretta's story. "It's interesting he didn't marry her. Usually exploiters marry," Goldman notes. But there had been no marriage, not because Taw didn't want it, but because Loretta wouldn't have it—she'd written in her journals that they pretended to be married, but had never tied the knot because of the "insecurity" of Taw's inventions.

Goldman stresses that the guilt Loretta's family has been working through—the woulda, coulda, shoulda—is misplaced. Unless they'd wanted to declare Loretta incompetent, or she'd sought a conservatorship to put all her assets in the hands of a guardian, there was little to be done. "Loretta was independent and lucid, and wasn't incapacitated," Goldman notes. There's not a whole lot anyone can do, except try to convince the person to leave. And Loretta had been adamant that "it's none of your business." She knew that would shut up her sisters, who'd been taught to "keep peace in the family at any cost."

Terri was in an even more precarious position—she'd already fought back against Taw and lost. Again and again. Her mother had made it clear that in any contest, Taw was the winner. How many times do you go back, looking to get beaten up all over again? Besides, she never thought Taw was violent.

But while Terri and everyone else was looking for bruises on the outside, they missed the bruises on the inside.

"Of all the forms of elder abuse, emotional or psychological abuse may be the most insidious and damaging," says Dr. David Helgeson, a clinical geropsychologist in private practice in Scottsdale. "Most of us have heard the childhood rhyme, 'Sticks and stones may break my bones, but words will never harm me.' As we all know, this is simply a defense against what is really true—words carry great power and hurt very deeply. The word *sarcasm*, for example, has its roots in a word that can literally be translated as 'intending to cut or render the flesh.' "

Dr. Helgeson says one powerful word signals abuse: "The name of the game is control, wherein the abuser assumes power over the elder, and the victims are then humiliated or made to feel inadequate."

You can often see this in the behavioral changes in the person being abused, experts say. If people who were open and happy become fearful and withdrawn; if sociable people become isolated and depressed; if people who normally shared their thoughts become hesitant to talk or even non-responsive—all those are red flags that something is terribly wrong.

You have to watch for the signs, because the person being abused isn't likely to admit it. They're most likely to go out of their way to hide it. Just like Loretta.

That leaves the frustrating question, "What can we do?" Domestic violence expert Ann Jones attacked that question directly in her book, *Next Time She'll Be Dead: Battering and How to Stop It*, published in 2000 by Beacon Press in Boston. Jones is herself the daughter of "a drunk, a wife beater and a child abuser." She never knew Loretta, but she could have been talking directly to her when she wrote:

Women should listen to their own uneasiness—and get more information about male violence and control. Al-

though no test is foolproof, there are early warning signs to watch for in behavior of any potential partner. . . . What is his attitude toward women? . . . How does he treat your women friends? Does he understand that they are as important to you as he is? (Do you understand that yourself?) What is his attitude toward your autonomy? . . . Does he tell you he'll take care of you? . . . Does he want to spend every minute with you? . . .

Stay away from a man who . . . wants or needs you intensely and exclusively, and who has a knack for getting his own way almost all the time. Any of the above should put you on guard. And if, when you back off, he turns on the solid gold charm, keep backing.

Terri learned all this in the days and weeks and months she searched for her mother. And she reacted to it like she had at other times of stress and unhappiness in her life—she turned to her business skills.

This time, she created a new business in honor of her mother. "Still N Style" is a shop she opened next to her Tempe consignment store during the year her mother was missing. It sells everything a woman needs to get on with life—clothing, household items, small appliances. Its first merchandise was everything Terri cleaned out of Loretta's home on Manhattan Drive. All Loretta's beautiful clothes filled racks in the new shop. Her lovely furniture and silver and glassware filled the shelves. Her paintings hung on its walls. Terri kept her jewelry and sent mementos to her brother and aunts and to her mother's friends, but everything else became the foundation for this new shop.

Then she announced that proceeds from Still N

Style would feed the Loretta Bowersock Fund, which would assist agencies devoted to helping abused elder women.

The first contributions went to DOVES. When it opened in the summer of 2004, it was the only shelter in the nation devoted to elder abuse victims.

Their slogan is chilling: "The golden years should not be black and blue." And the stories that come to the shelter with these elderly victims are heartbreaking. "We've had women completely disowned by their kids because they finally spoke up and sought help," says DOVES director Alice Ghareib. "Remember, if Mom leaves Dad, that shifts responsibility for them to adult children. So they hear, 'Come on now, why rock the boat after forty-three years of marriage?'; or they hear, 'Come on, you've lived long enough with him to know how to handle him.' "

Oftentimes, Ghareib notes, these are women who have devoted their entire lives to raising and caring for a family. When do their needs ever come first? It's no surprise they don't see that now, either. Perhaps there are religious vows to deal with, and cultural considerations, and besides, they have no idea where to go if they don't stay home and take it.

"This generation for the most part didn't work outside the home," Ghareib notes. "They have no Social Security of their own, no pension of their own, no job skills of their own. Some of them have difficulty even admitting they're victims of domestic violence. They think it just means he hits you, and so they wonder if the emotional or exploitive abuse they're suffering really is abuse at all."

Most of them have no idea that the abuse they're suffering, under Arizona law, is criminal.

Since January of 2003, the Phoenix Police Department has gone after late life abuse with its Vulnerable Adult Crimes Unit, which is headed by Detective Ted Evertsen. He says he only knows of one other police department in the country that has such a focus, and that's in San Diego. "The Southwest is the leader in this," he says, reflecting both the aging population already there and the giant baby boomer population reaching its sixties.

Detective Evertsen has a potent piece of advice for anyone who suspects that a loved one is being abused: "Don't talk yourself out of it. Don't say, 'Oh, there's probably nothing wrong, it's just my imagination.' If you suspect something is wrong, it probably is. It's good to be a little suspicious, to snoop around."

And, he adds, do not be derailed if the victim becomes defensive, as Loretta always did when anyone tried to intercede. "I hope more and more people become aware, because this is going to get bigger," Detective Evertsen says.

It fits hand-in-glove that the first city to have a police unit devoted to elder abuse is also the first city to have a shelter for elder victims.

The DOVES complex came about because the Area Agency on Aging found a desperate need while seeing that regular shelters didn't work. They had first set up a hot line where older women could call to report problems and ask for help. But when they sent those women to the existing shelters, there were problems. "The dynamics of domestic violence are the same no matter how old you are, but how women experience them and the degree they experience them is different," Ghareib says.

Regular shelters are often two-story buildings, usually house women and their children in communal rooms with several bunk beds, and require everyone to do chores. None of that works for an older woman.

"If there are stairs, forget it," Ghareib notes. "Elder victims are more comfortable in small, private rooms without the noise and activity of children. Hallways are not always wide enough to accommodate walkers, nor do they have grab bars in the bath, or raised toilet seats. These women are also more comfortable talking in groups of women like themselves. We found that elderly victims had special needs."

So the agency went looking for a one-story apartment complex that could be turned into a shelter. Like the women they were trying to save, the building they found was an old, worn-down and abused place to give a new life to. "The paint was chipping, the plumbing was rusty, the units were filled with soiled carpets, the landscaping had been let go completely and the pool was greener than the grass," remembers Wally Sjolander, senior vice president of the Area Agency on Aging. But the twenty-unit complex in central Phoenix—a U-shaped development around a slimy pool—was just perfect.

The woman who owned the complex lived out of state, but sympathized with the plan and agreed to rent the complex until the agency could get financing in place. Another angel was Phoenix council member Peggy Bilsten, who helped get $1 million in city housing funds. The Arizona State Housing Trust Fund kicked in $300,000 for remodeling, and they found a whole chorus of angels to help get the place in shape.

Master Builder Gary Gietz donated $30,000 worth of remodeling to make one unit a "community center" where residents gather for group meetings, socializing and communal holiday dinners. They got grants from the Virginia G. Piper and Nina Mason Pulliam Charitable Trusts. Students in the interior design school at Scottsdale Community College decorated each bungalow and donated all the furnishings. Sears donated over half the appliances for the units. Paddock Pools renovated the pool at cost. Multicom installed alarm systems. At Thanksgiving, food boxes arrived from Tanner Chapel AME Church. The Phoenix Civitans prepared and served Christmas dinners. The Trilogy Quilters from a retirement community in Gilbert made quilts for each woman who sought peace here.

And then came Terri Bowersock with her new business and her commitment to help. She announced the pledge at a second memorial held for her mother, on January 19, 2006.

Terri says at first she thought of just having a few close friends to the house to say a final good-bye to Loretta—before she took her ashes to Hawaii to scatter them with Scott—but so many people wanted and needed the closure of a service.

So instead, she held the memorial in the new Still N Style shop that was under construction. Plastic chairs were set up amidst its particleboard shelves yet to be painted, its drywall yet to be textured. Makeshift tables held a cake and chafing dishes with nibbles.

Terri called it a "celebration of life" and about 100 people showed up—the "band of sisters" who'd walked the desert with her and held her hand through it all; the psychics who'd shared their visions; friends from over the years; family associates.

The memorial was filled with love and laughter, a few tears, and hundreds of pictures to attest to the lively, classy lady who was Loretta Jean McJilton Bowersock. There was a black-and-white picture of Loretta holding baby Terri, and wearing a dress and earrings that could have come right out of Lucille Ball's wardrobe for *I Love Lucy*. There was Loretta as a young mother with her husband, son and daughter. There was Loretta in her tennis togs, and with her five sisters, and with Terri on a beach when they last visited Scott, and with Taw on that last trip to Alaska.

There was a letter from Loretta to Terri:

Thanks for making me famous. Now I'm known as "Terri's Mom."

"We were just at the place where we were going to travel and shop and have a good time with the money," Terri told the crowd. "I always said someday we'd go shopping on Rodeo Drive, but my mother absolutely adored consignment shopping and she'd never have paid retail!" The audience laughed at that, and there was a twinge of pain to think of a daughter who had hoped her money would impress her mom enough to pay the dreaded mark-up prices.

But besides paging through the photo albums of all the happy times, there was a final album with the sad pictures. The gravesite. The rocks. The blue motel. The Reverend Kathryn McDowell looked over the crowd: "Quite a village has built around this situation," she said, and then looked at Terri: "The essence of who Loretta was is alive in Terri."

One friend got up and pointed out that the white plastic chairs friends had lent for the occasion were factory-imprinted with the word "Loretta" on the back—"Now how in the world did *this* happen?" he asked the astonished crowd.

"The things I got to learn this year were absolutely phenomenal," Terri told them. "What I'm learning about goodness and love—sometimes I feel my mother is holding my hand."

And the biggest thing she learned is that she couldn't bear to think of her mother as just another statistic—just another elder abuse victim who lived in fear.

She announced her support for DOVES and handed out brochures on the agency, hoping her friends would support it, too.

Terri told the gathered friends that she spent a lot of time talking to her mother since Loretta disappeared. "I hear her voice all the time. When you love someone, you're always talking to them," she said. Sometimes, she added, her mother answers back. "I asked her, 'Are you with Taw?' and she said, '*Oh no*, he's on another level.'"

But the memorial brought out the media's fangs—at

least privately in newsrooms around the Valley. "She had it at her *store*, like she was doing an ad for her place," one journalist at Channel 3 complained. Donna Rossi of Channel 5 remembers hearing the same kind of grumbling in her newsroom. "It made perfect sense to me, because she was dedicating the store to her mom and to DOVES," Rossi says. But even some of Terri's friends had to agree with the buzz that this was over the top. As one put it, "The first memorial was wonderful, but Loretta wouldn't have wanted the second one. It didn't feel right."

Whatever the complaints behind the scenes, the memorial spotlighted DOVES, bringing it its first real publicity. In the first year-and-a-half, Terri donated $50,000 from her store to DOVES, and another $75,000 to the Fresh Start foundation, which deals with an entire range of abused women's issues.

The financial commitment came even as Terri struggled to keep her business afloat. By the time she came back from her year-long desert searches and started focusing on her business full-time, it was in shambles. She discovered she had to build it up all over again. "Buckle down," she told her staff, and they did.

Meanwhile, her Web site, www.shopterris.com, was expanded to raise money for abused women. "I want to devote the rest of my life to creating a charity eBay to help women," she says.

"You can still hear her voice change when she talks about her mother," her friend Karen Stone says. "I heard her give a speech, and there was Terri being all Terri, and when she got to her mom, she sounded so differently. I don't think she'll ever get over this."

What she is over—and what seems most remarkable to many who have watched this story—is her anger toward Taw. She even held a small, intimate memorial for him in her back yard after Loretta's body was found.

Most find it incomprehensible that she could have anything but hatred for the man who stole her mother. Her aunts say they'll never forgive him, and most of her friends share that emotion. But Terri has "let go," as she puts it.

"A lot of people said, 'I hate that man. He's so evil. How could you even think about forgiving him?' But I just knew I had to," she said in a Sonja Haller column printed in the *Arizona Republic* in 2006, which focused on the theme of "forgiveness." It was that time of year, both for Christians, who were celebrating Easter, and for Jews, who had begun Passover that week.

"I don't want to walk through the rest of my life angry and mad," Terri is quoted as saying. "I thought, 'I could spend my life paying attention to him and what he did, or I can forgive him.'"

The article continued:

Bowersock said she couldn't begin to forgive Benderly until she forgave herself. She mentally listed and then let go of the would-haves, could-haves, should-haves. She read her mother's journal after her death and learned that Benderly had been psychologically abusing her for years. "Why didn't I see what was happening?" Bowersock said.

"Why didn't I take her out of the house? Why did I con-done this?" Bowersock said she became aware of her in-ternal dialogue. She would blame herself, then jump to her own defense, saying what's done is done and that it wouldn't bring her mother back. "I would just stop those thoughts and get to the good [ones]," she said. Therapists call that breaking the cycle of obsessive thoughts. Like-wise, people must break loose from a loop of thoughts about how they were betrayed, hurt or insulted.

The story noted that Benderly had been abused as a child, and quoted Terri as responding:

"It doesn't condone the murder. But I was able to look at Taw and see that maybe there was something inside his chromosomes and a whole bunch of pain in his own life that might have been some of the reason he did what he did."

Terri told Haller she had one main reason for for-giving Taw:

"I want to be happy. It's about giving yourself permis-sion to be happy in the present moment. I had to forgive to do that."

But later, when she thought about it, she realized there was another reason that trumped everything else: "I have absolutely let go of my anger. I'm not going to spend my time on that. He had taken so much time from her when she was alive, I'm not going to let him have any time now."

She'd rather spend the time thinking of her mother, working to help other women and getting on with life.

"She's with me a lot," Terri says. "I'm actually having a better relationship with my mother now than before. Boy, did I love her. I can't wait to die— the first thing I'll do is run into her arms. I now know she loves me—I didn't know it before. When she was alive, I never felt I did enough."

EPILOGUE

I was in North Dakota visiting my own precious parents on a Christmas holiday when Terri lost her mother in 2004. I didn't even know about it until I returned home to Phoenix in January. And there she was, on the evening news, and I almost levitated off the couch—how could this be happening to someone I knew?

I rushed to my computer and sought out the archives of the *Arizona Republic* and read the first stories in horror. Her mother was "missing," and presumed dead and buried somewhere in the Arizona desert. I thought I was going to be sick.

I called Terri and, although she sounded tired, it was still that voice that was so familiar. We weren't close friends, but I knew her from the TV commercials and from my days at Channel 3—she was a frequent guest on our morning show, where I did political commentary. We'd giggled together the day she came on to tell about her appearance on *Oprah*. I'd also seen her at fund-raisers around town, and had always found her energy and spunk enticing. She told me what was happening then—Taw had already committed suicide and the desert searches were continuing, but nothing had been found.

I couldn't get her out of my mind. I'm exceptionally close to my mother, and I knew Terri had been close to hers. My mother, Willie, is the single most important person in my life, always has been, always will be. I can't even imagine the day I'll lose her. I feel like a totally blessed child that I still have both her and my dad, now in their mid-80s.

What if someone stole her from me? What if someone hurt her, and made her suffer? What if someone tossed her out in the desert somewhere with the snakes and eagles and coyotes and buzzards? The thought was so horrifying, I couldn't get it out of my mind. The next day, the *Arizona Republic* ran another story on Terri's futile search, and in her words I heard strength and resolve. I wondered if I'd have such poise if it were happening to me and my mother.

I called her back a few days later and told her I wanted to write about what she was going through: what had happened, why it had happened, and what we could learn from this. She was most interested in the last point—"Oh, Jana, you can't believe what we've learned. I don't know how I couldn't have seen it." And then she started telling me the whole story—a story she hadn't shared with anyone else.

I've been an Arizona journalist since 1972. I'm a Midwest girl who grew up in North Dakota and went West after earning my master's degree at the University of Michigan. I've worked for the *Arizona Republic*, for the alternative weekly *New Times*, for public television, and for a commercial TV station. Since 2001, I've been freelancing, writing a column and features for *Phoenix*, the monthly city magazine in Arizona's capital. After talking with Terri, I emailed my editor at the time, Robert Stieve. I told him a little of what Terri had relayed, and he instantly emailed back, encouraging me to pursue the story and promising to devote as much space to it as I needed.

And that's how the journey began that has resulted in this book. My first feature for *Phoenix* magazine was in June of 2005: "Where Is My Mother's Body?" It was the first time Terri's anguishing background story was told: the break in her relationship with her mother, her mother's betrayal, the anger at—and the awesome extent of—Taw's control. We had talked for hours and hours, and she spilled it all out, as though finally telling the entire story was a way to step out of her grieving robes.

I left her beautiful Ahwatukee home after our first interview and didn't turn north toward Phoenix, but south on Interstate 10 to the I-8 cutoff. As I drove the same road Taw had driven on his way to Tucson, I tried to see what he had seen, tried to imagine what he'd been thinking. As I turned onto the "San Diego cutoff," I saw a cemetery just off the road a ways. I passed by, driving miles down the highway and off into the desert, now and then struck by the thought: Oh God, the desert is so incredibly vast and secretive, how are they ever going to find Loretta?

I turned back and found myself drawn to the Casa Grande Cemetery. It was filled with all the love and care and extravagance familiar to a Mexican graveyard. I spent a couple of hours there, trying to figure out how long it had been around; reading the gravestones and messages left by families, and noticing the decorations and trinkets left behind to mark the special joys and pleasures of the dead. At one point, I came upon a couple who were kneeling by a grave. They told me his father had just died and they came every day after work to visit the grave, and invited me to pray with them. I did, and thought how wonderful that a son could devote such time to honoring his father. He thought I was crying for his dad, and I let him think that. But I was crying for Terri, because she could never do this. There was no grave for her. No place to decorate or visit or know her mother was safe. The enormity of that heartbreak settled like a fog.

I wrote a second story after Loretta's body was found, running in *Phoenix* magazine in April of 2006. "He Buried My Mother by a Blue Motel," it was titled. By then, Terri was already spreading the word about a new wrinkle in the domestic violence picture—elder abuse.

I've written extensively about domestic violence for years, although I prefer to call it what it really is: assault and battery. I don't like that we "nice it up" by pretending violence at home is somehow different from violence on the street—to me, it's even more brutal, more cruel, because trust and love are beaten up and destroyed, too.

A series of stories I wrote for *New Times* weekly in 1989 helped change many of Arizona's laws to get tough on abusers. And perhaps the proudest day of my professional life was in 2001 when I helped get a woman out of prison—she'd already served thirteen of an absurd twenty years for killing her abusive husband in self-defense. For almost two decades, fighting domestic abuse has been the charity I donate my time and name to.

But now I was learning about a new focus, and of course, Arizona was in the forefront—one year, next to Mississippi, we were the state with the highest number of women dying at the hands of men who said they loved them. We consistently rank in the top ten of domestic violence deaths.

The very first shelter in the nation devoted to elder abuse victims had opened in Phoenix, and Terri announced that she had created a new business to help support it. Loretta's death would not be just another statistic—Terri was determined it would help wake people up and give women new hope.

I found that very compelling. So I started researching elder abuse and was aghast at what I found. That led to more stories and more resolve to spotlight this problem.

Some fifty interviews, thousands of pages of documents and hundreds of miles of desert driving later, this book is the result. At one point, my dear friend, Marge Injasoulian, spent a long day with me retracing every step of the journey from Loretta's house to the site of her grave. We went to the shops Taw had gone to; went to the truck stop where he'd bought sandwiches; marveled at all the blue at the motel he'd passed; drove down the wash he'd traveled to the grave; even met the whiskered desert loner who lived nearby and warned us off going any farther.

I tried to follow this story wherever it went, finding insight from attorneys and business associates and family members and friends and psychics and journalists and sisters, and of course, Terri. She and I had dozens of telephone and in-person interviews. One night we sat in her living room and went through the boxes of her mother's personal journals. Every now and then I'd find an entry where her mother had written something loving about her, and I always read it out loud. I figured she could use all the mother hugs she could still get.

I moved to a lovely lake home near Brainerd, Minnesota, the summer of 2007 to write this book, choosing a place close to my family. As I wrote about the agony Terri and her family and friends had gone through—the unbelievable loss and the tenacious search—I was surrounded by those I love the most. My sister, Judy, had spent weeks getting the cabin ready, filling it with all the touches that made it "home." My mother Willie was there often, loving the beautiful forest and the pretty lake. My dad, Rudy, came a couple times and was a real champ, even though the fishing was lousy. My brothers, Gary and Duane, got married and brought their lovely brides, Susan and Jeanette, to the lake to honeymoon with the whole family—yes, we're close, and it's a hoot to honeymoon with your brothers! I admit it struck me as strange more than once that I was having such joy as I was writing about such sorrow.

When you start writing a book, you think you know what you're writing about. But you discover things along the way. You're not just reciting a story—the facts and nothing but the facts—but you're trying to make sense of it. I admit I had a helluva time making sense of Loretta and Taw. She drew such sympathy from me, but there were times she made me so angry—this beautiful, talented, competent woman, who put up with such a lout for so long because she didn't want to be alone. I'm wondering how many nights she lay in the dark and realized just how alone she was.

Taw was easier for me to understand, and I never could muster any sympathy for him. I've known men like that: men whose entire focus is their own self-interest and who can lie without blinking because they believe their own BS. He personified every awful trait a man can have, with none of the redeeming ones that make male behavior tolerable. He put up with all her gnashing of teeth and self-discovery crusades and screaming and fights because he had a cash cow who wouldn't leave him. She put up with him, why?

And here's what got me the most: How could she have allowed him to ruin her relationship with her daughter? How could she have taken his side and abandoned Terri? She wouldn't marry the man because he had no financial security, but she gave him such incredible control over her anyway. I know women acquiesce to men all the time—sometimes on demand, sometimes by tradition. But come on—there has to be a point when even the neediest woman draws the line.

My summer environment finally helped me understand. There were acres of corn fields on the county road to my cottage, and I watched the entire growing season as I was working on this book. Most of these crops are grown for silage, to feed cattle and pigs during the winter. "Field corn" they call it.

When I arrived in Brainerd at the end of June, the field corn was just poking out of the earth, just starting its stretch toward the sky. Everyone thinks the corn is fine if it's "knee high by the Fourth of July," and more than once I heard concerns that it better hurry. But by our nation's birthday, it fit the measure, and now folks were saying that if you sat in a corn field, you could hear it grow. Sometimes, driving down County Road 23, I thought I could see it grow.

But then came the fear that there wasn't enough rain for the corn to tassel, and if it didn't, there wouldn't be any ears and the crop would be lost. I watched the stalks wilt before the rain came that saved the day. But as summer gave way to fall in September, entire fields turned totally brown and dry and withered. My lifelong friend, Maxine Beckstrom, was visiting one weekend, and as we drove down that road, I remarked how sad it was that the corn had died like that. Maxine can't believe I grew up in North Dakota—even as a "town girl"—but never learned anything about farming, so she laughed and explained: "They can't harvest field corn until every bit of green is gone."

After that, every time I drove down that road, I thought how much those fields were like Loretta and Taw's relationship.

She didn't give up until every bit of green was gone, until there was nothing left but dry, brown, broken dreams. And when she tried to end it, he killed her.

He didn't give up until every bit of green was gone, either, taking the last of it out of the bank on his way out of town.

Some stories haunt you because there are so many times you can see a different ending.

This is one of them.

It's one that broke my heart.